I0443213

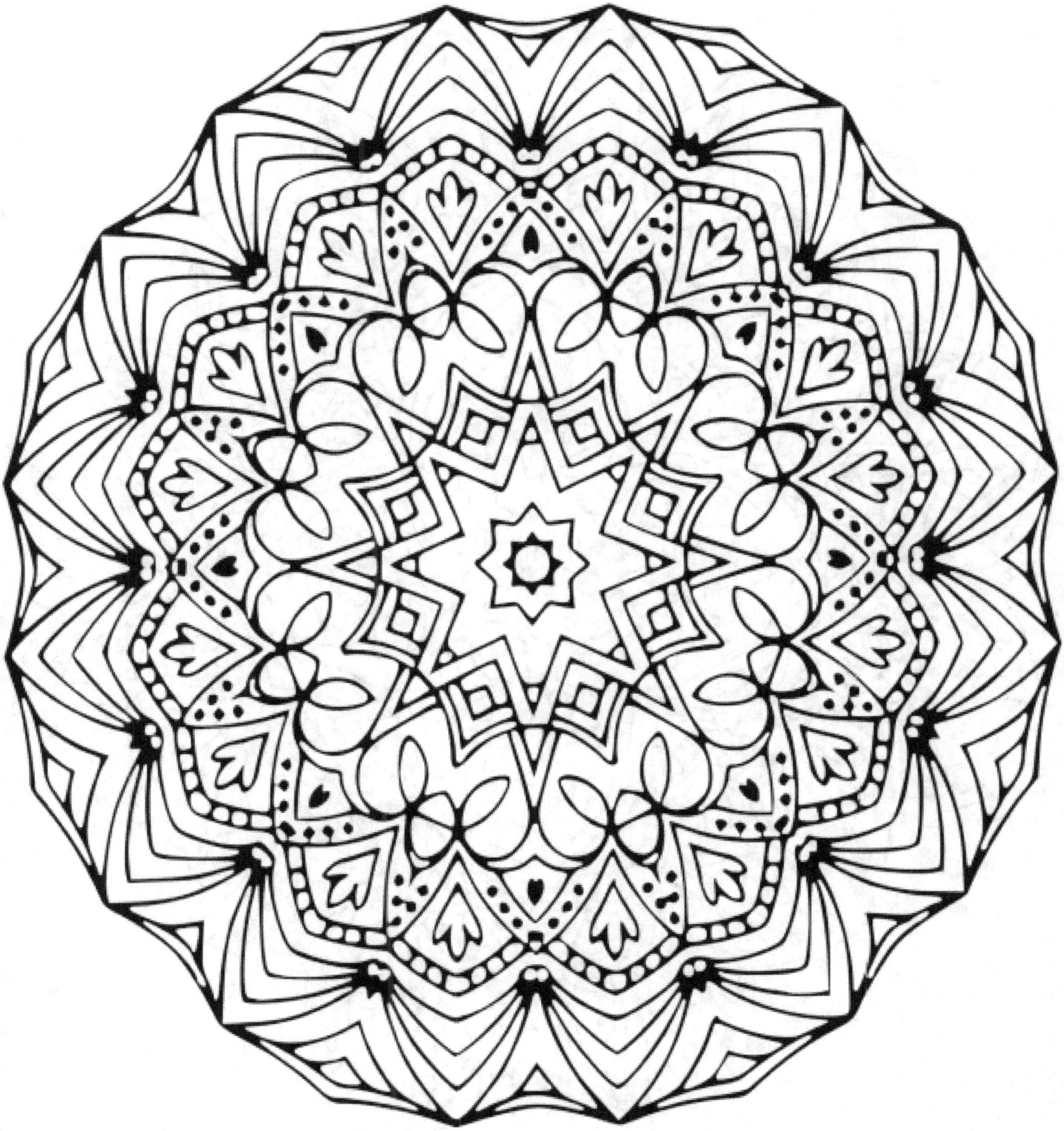

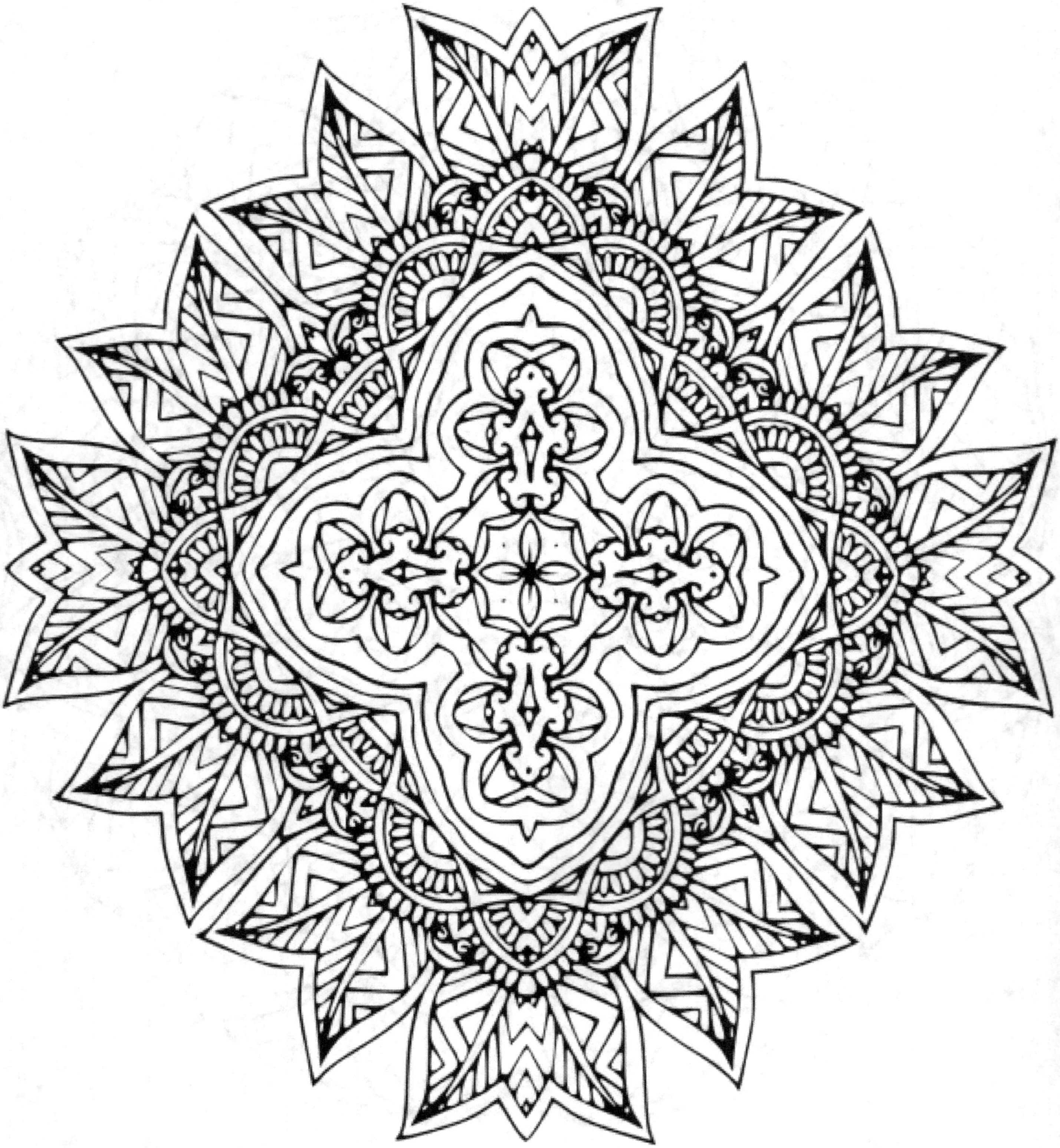

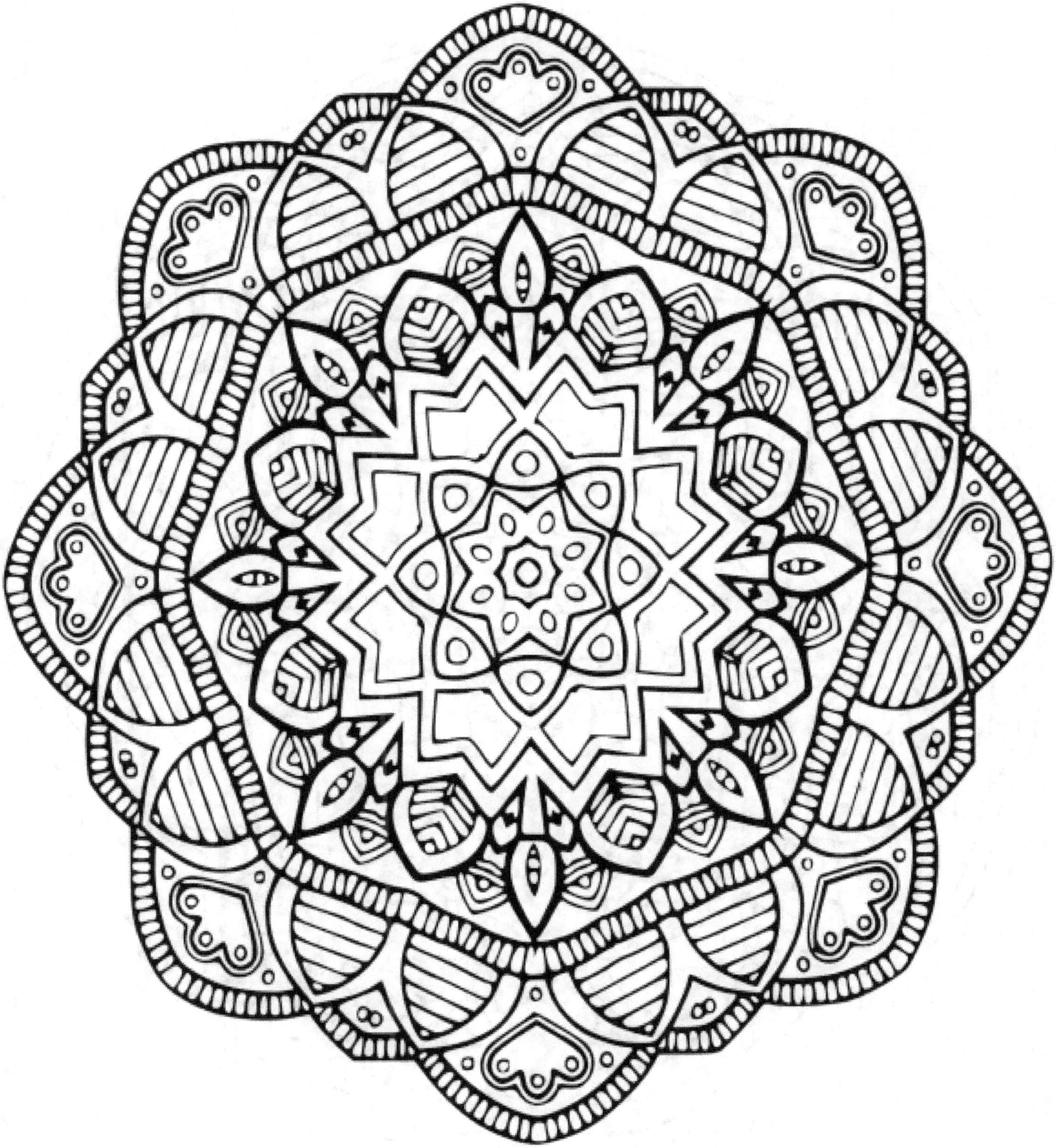

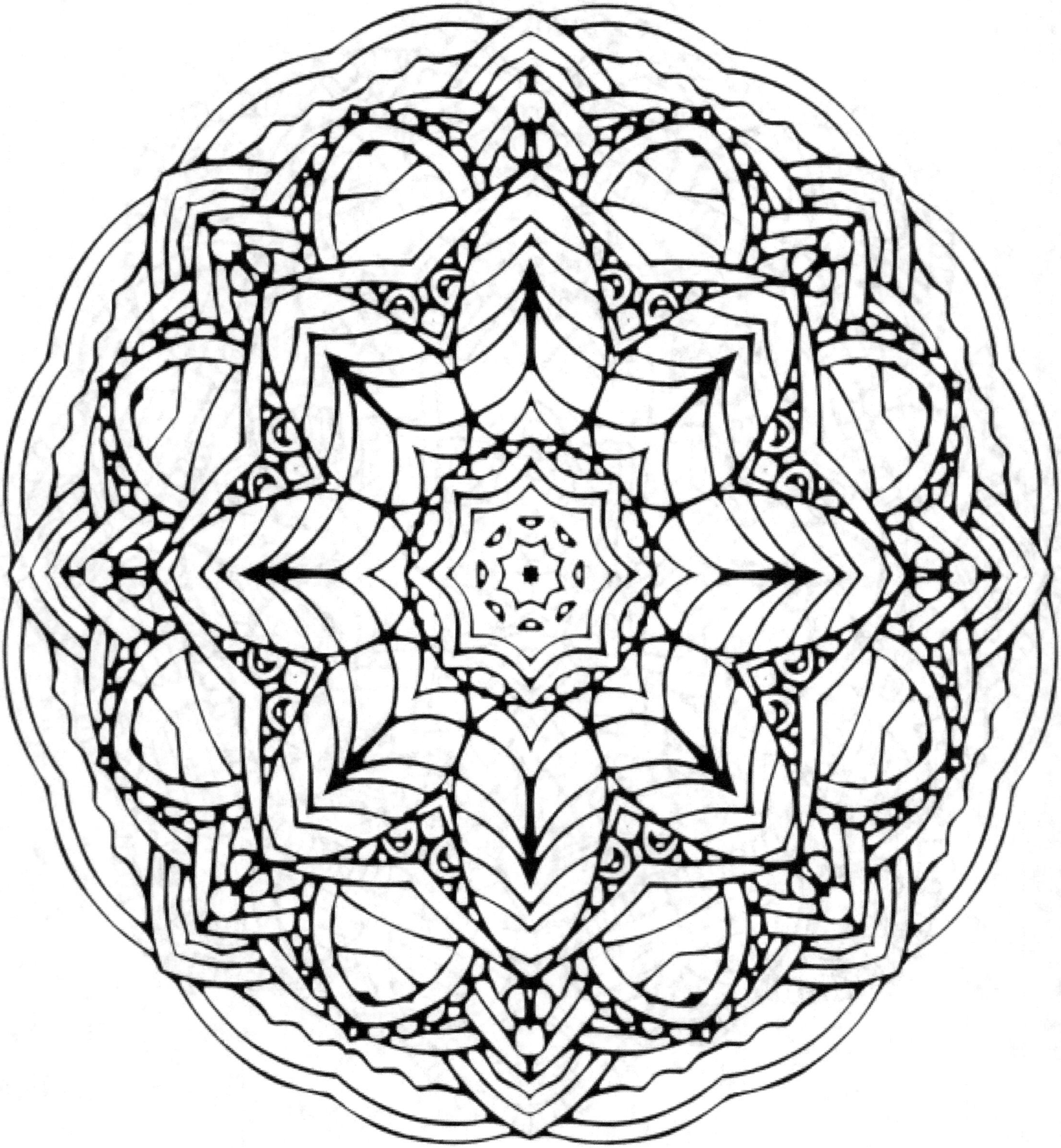

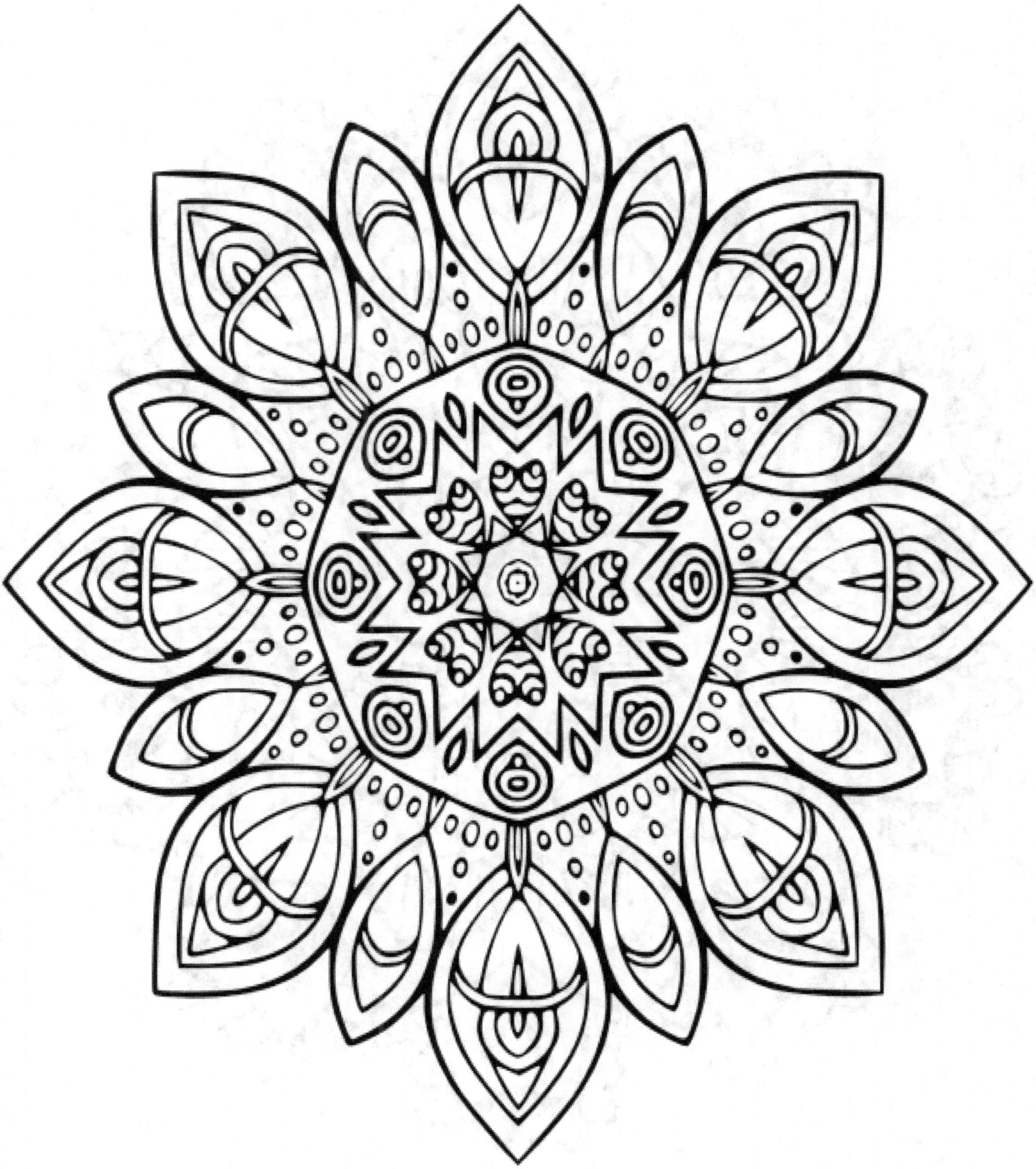

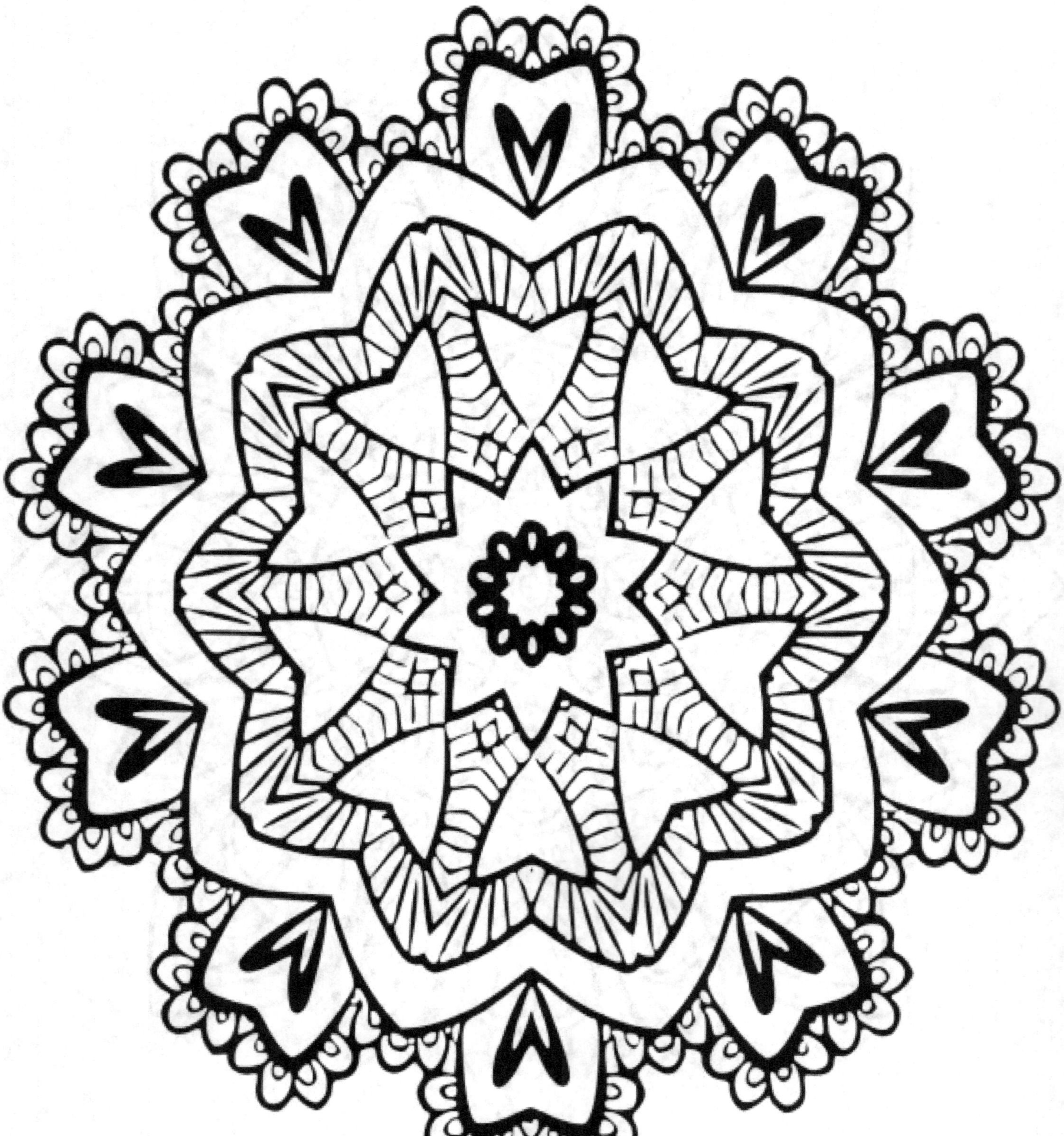

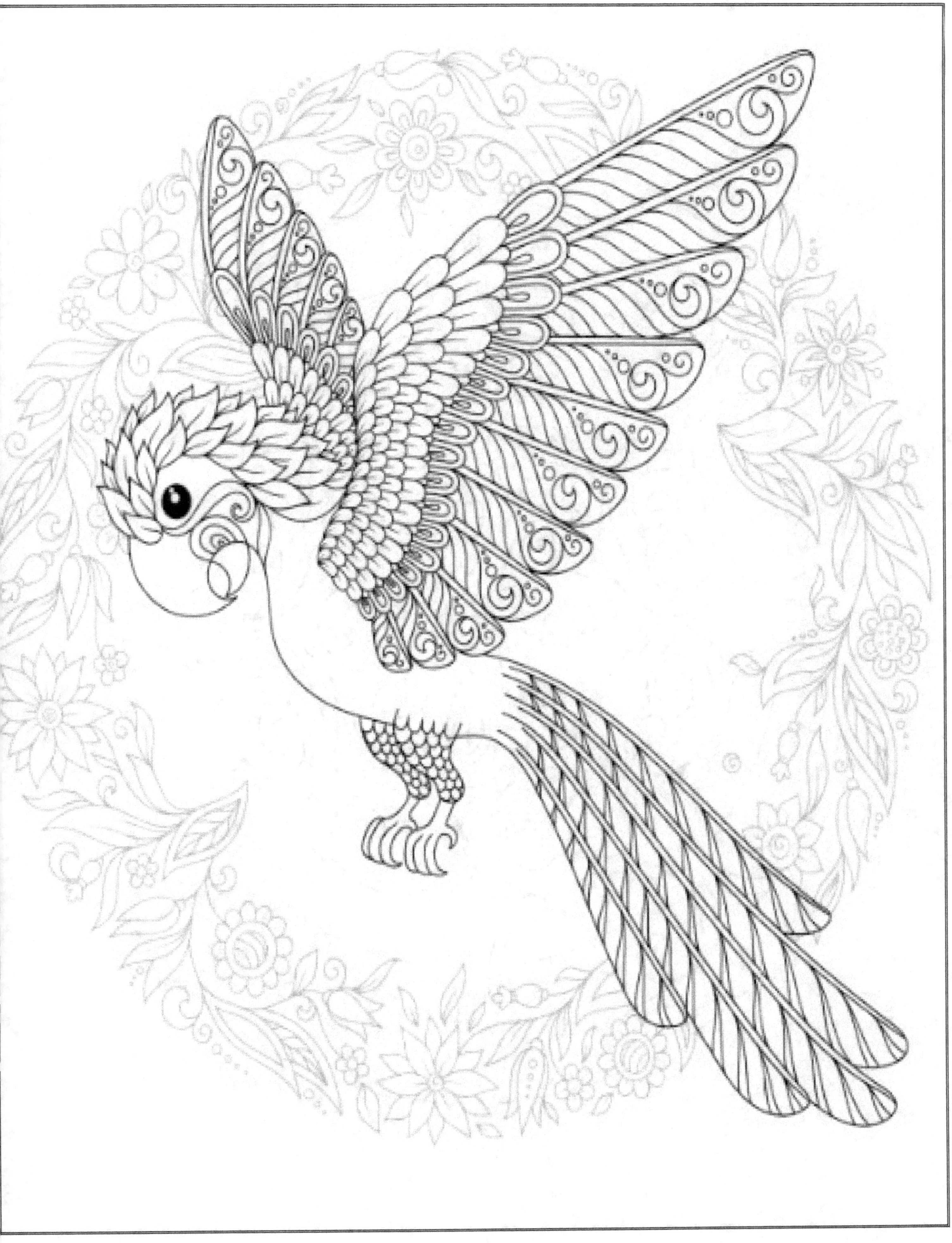

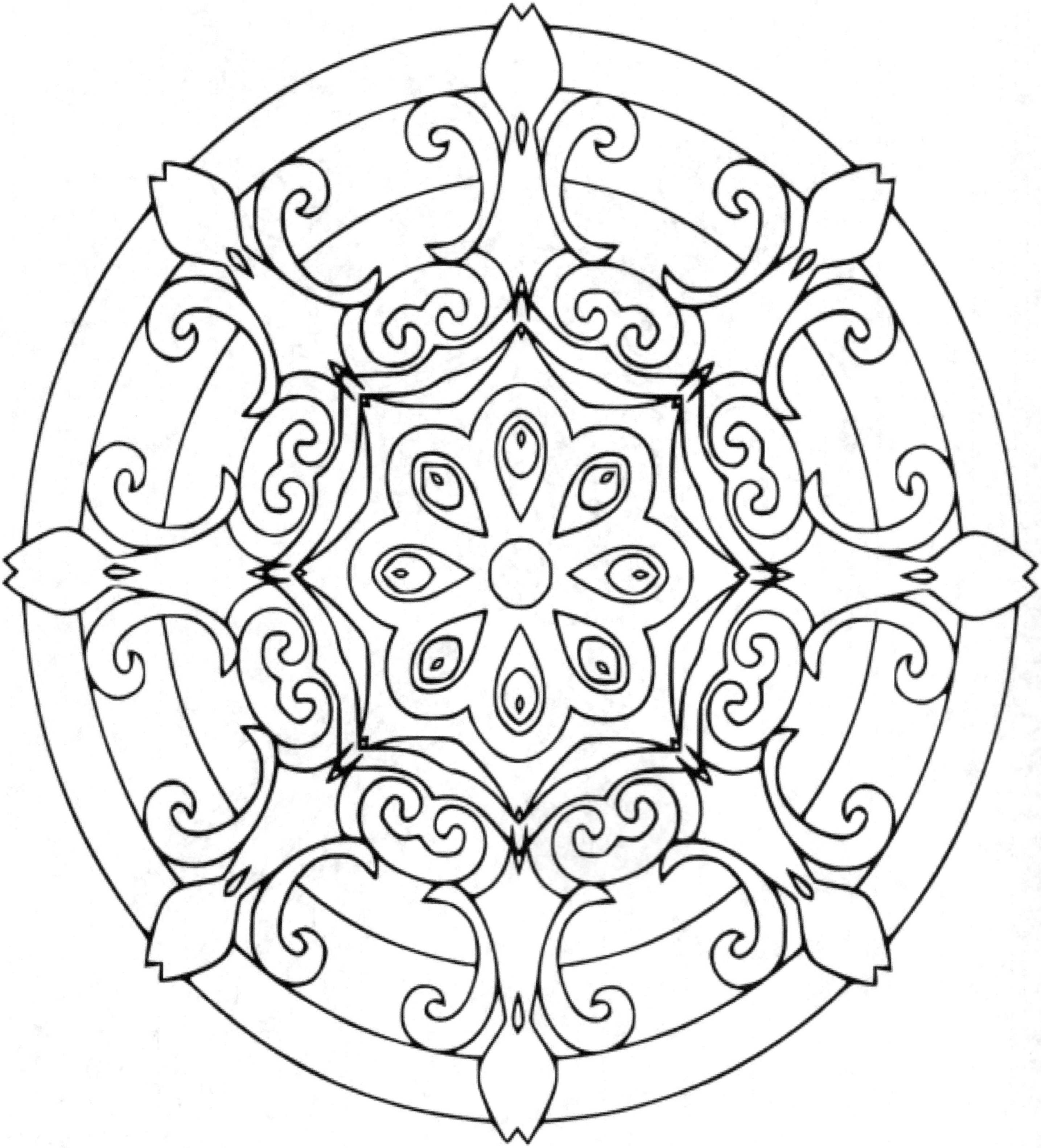

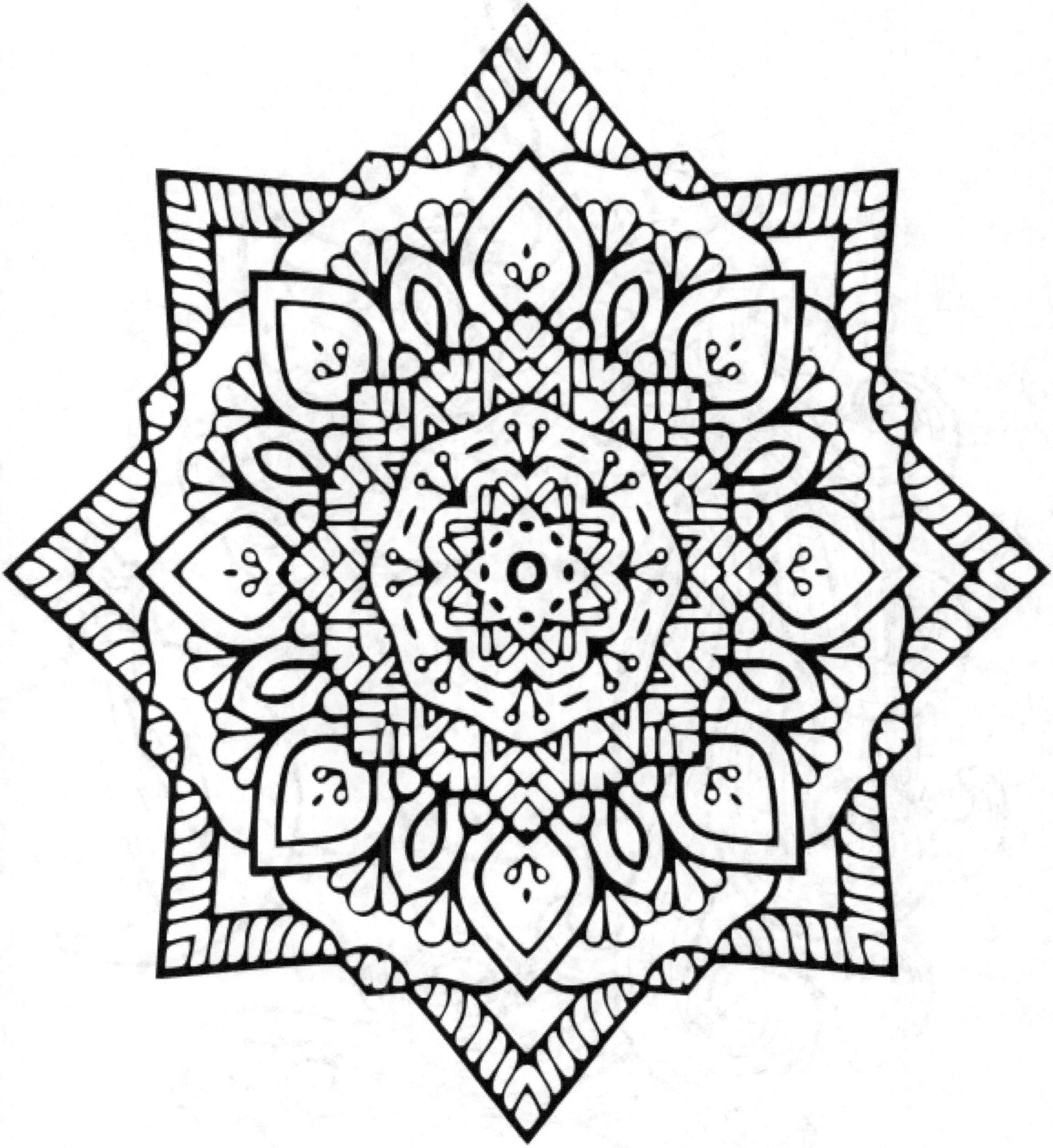

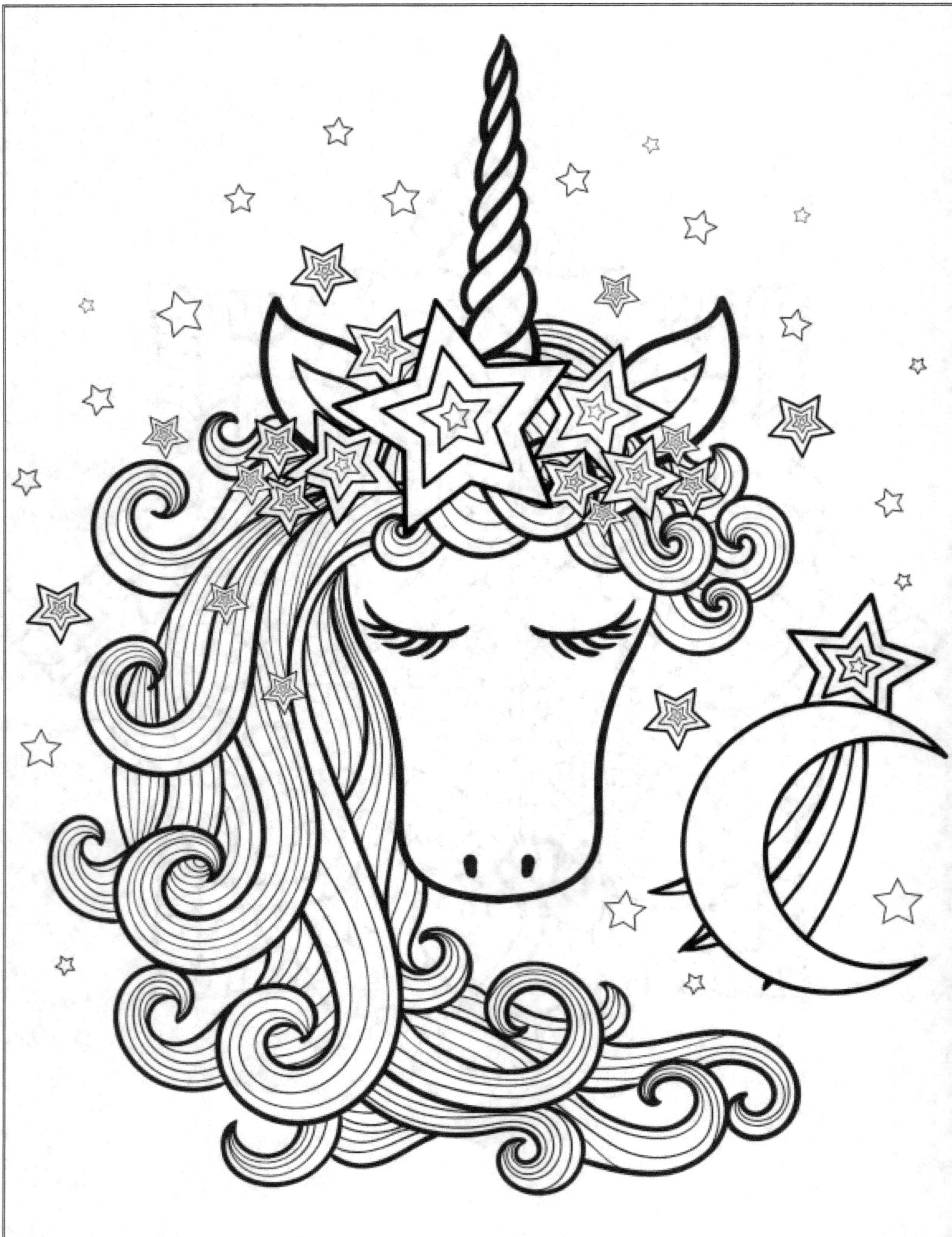

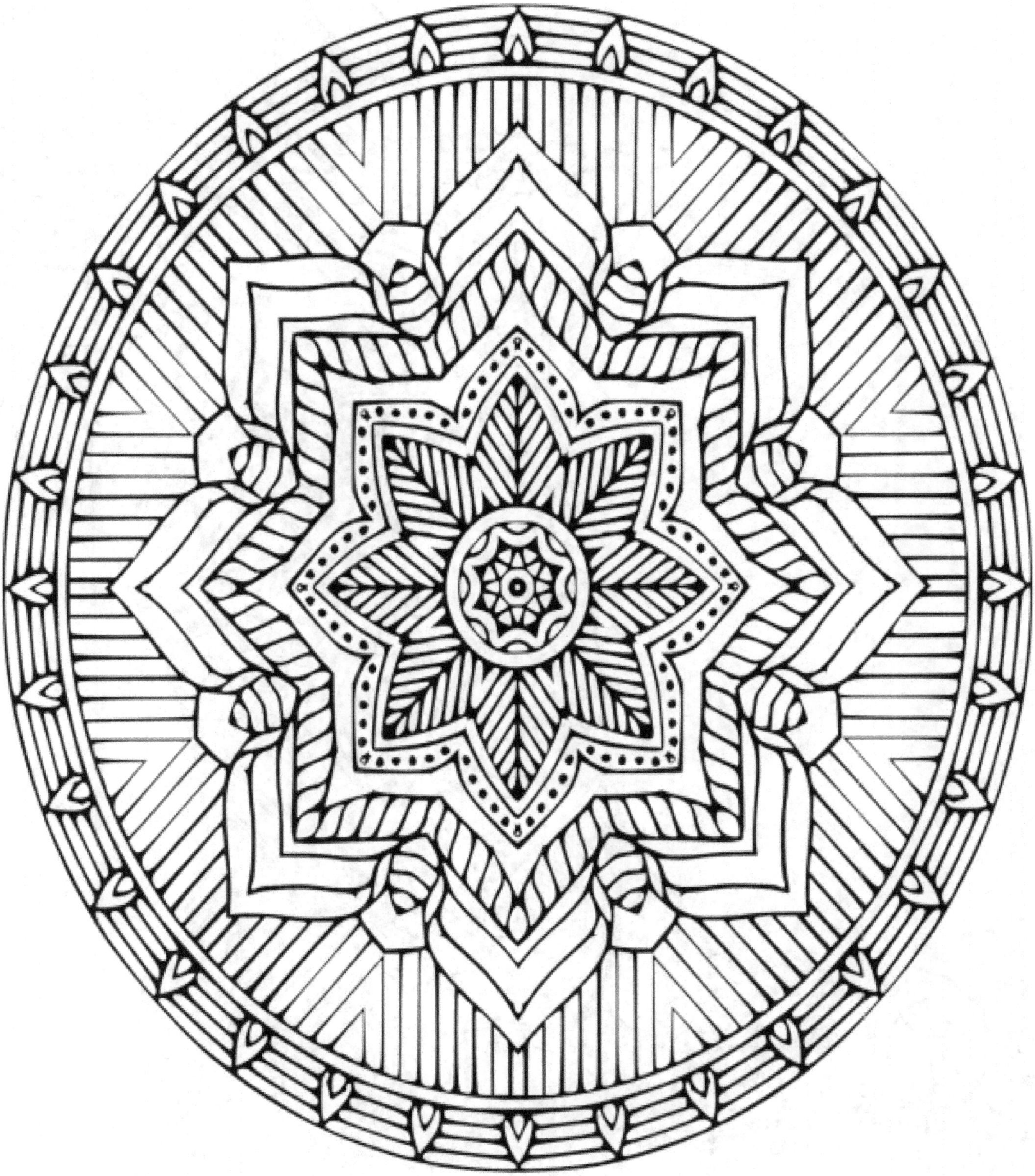

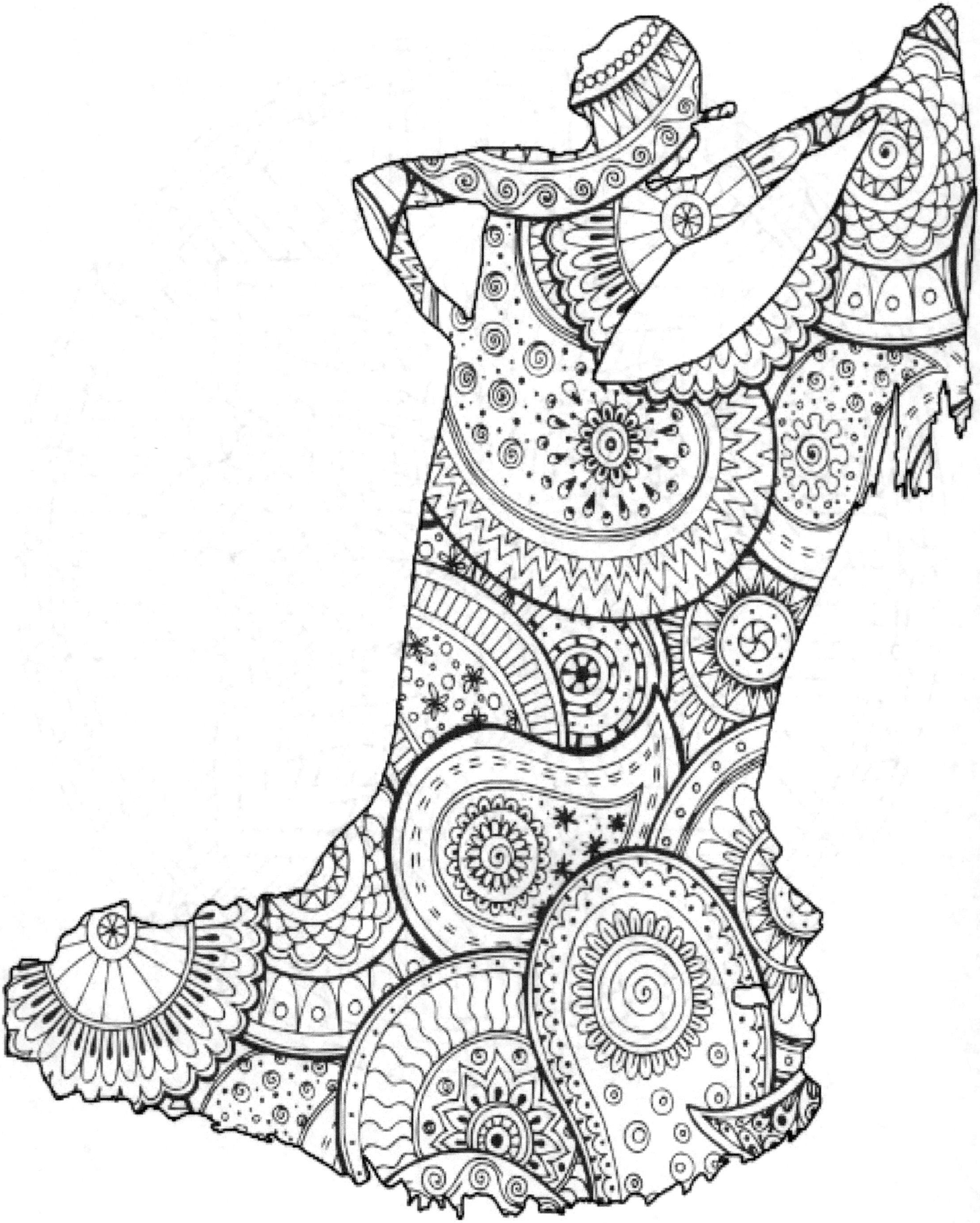

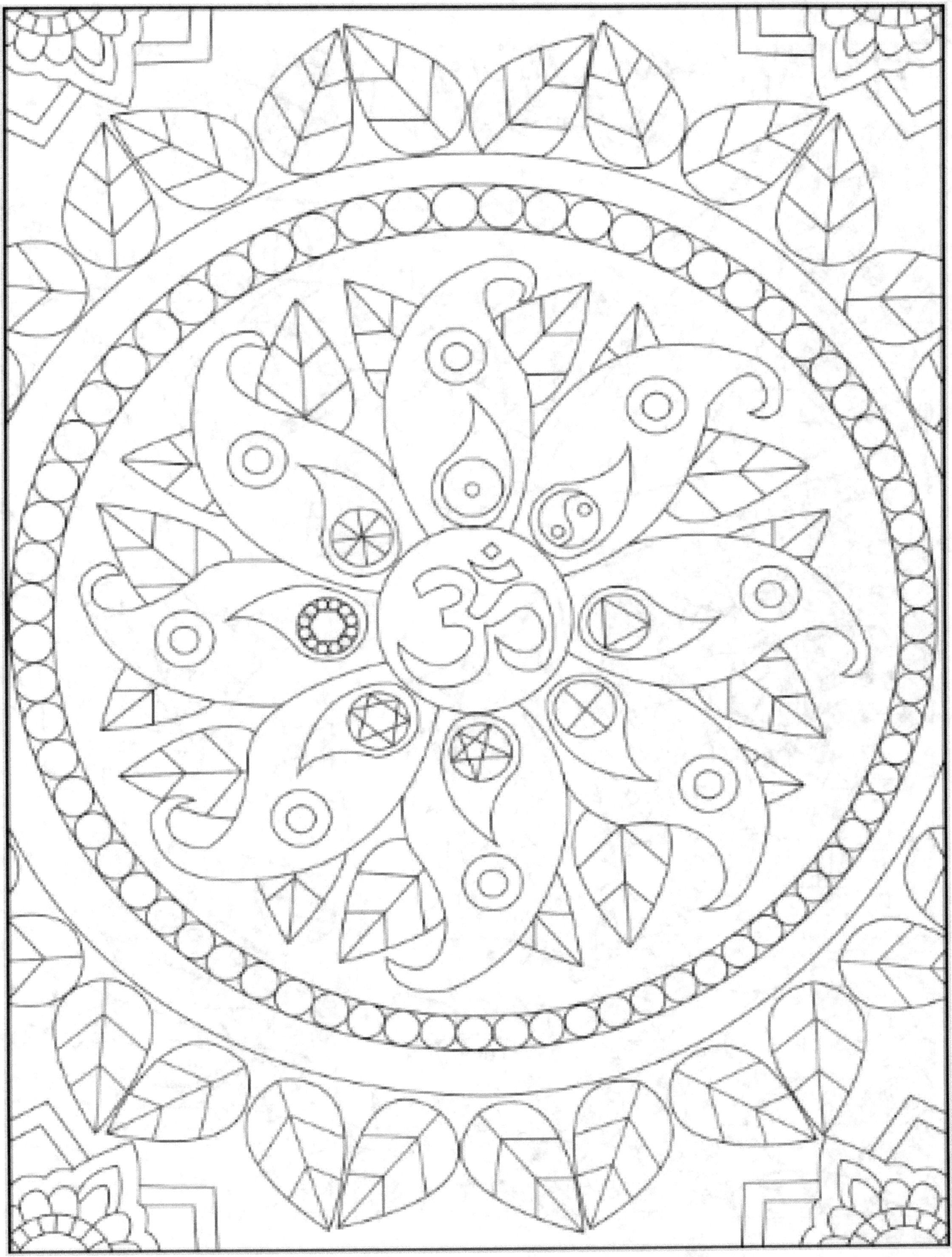

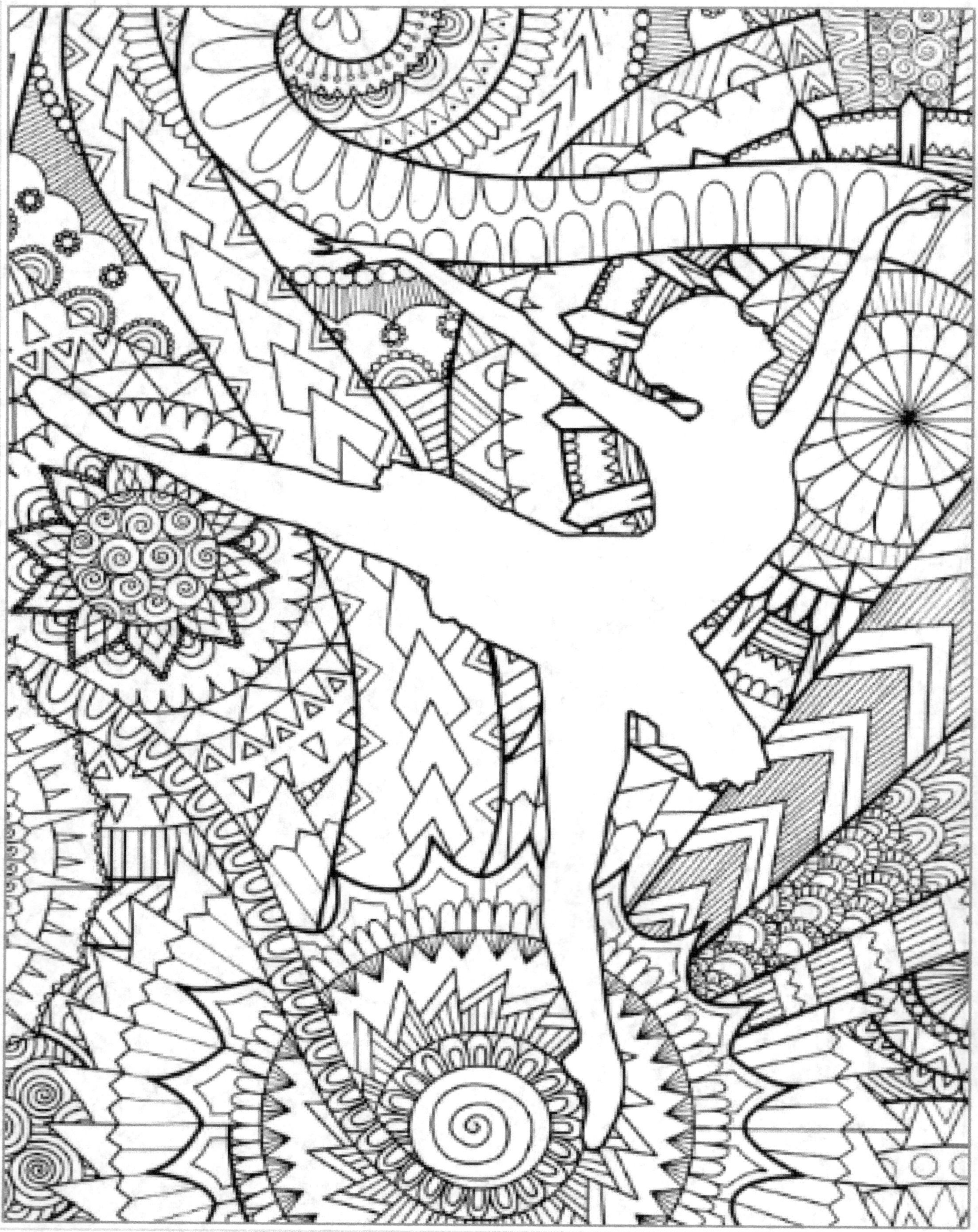

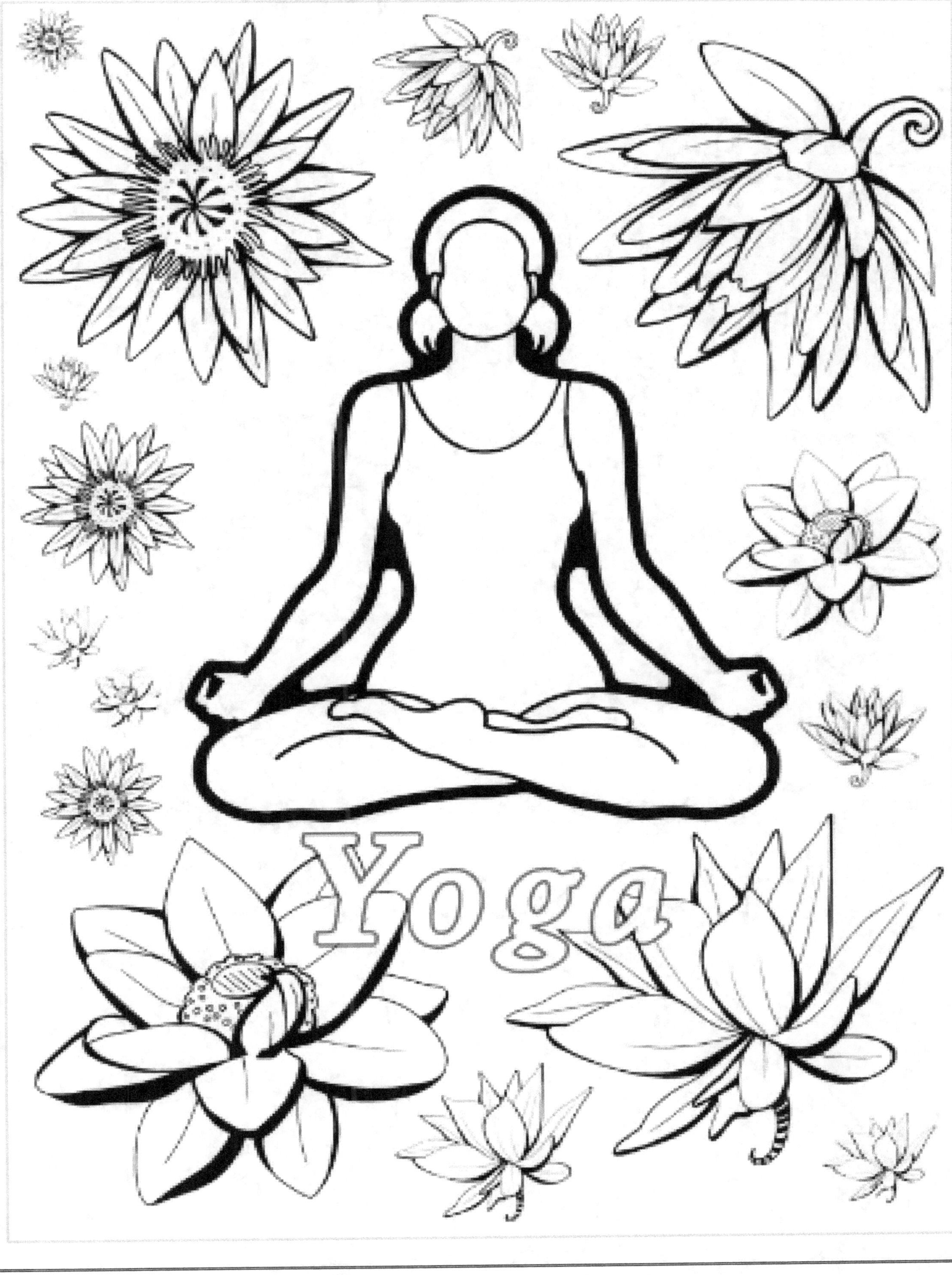
Yoga

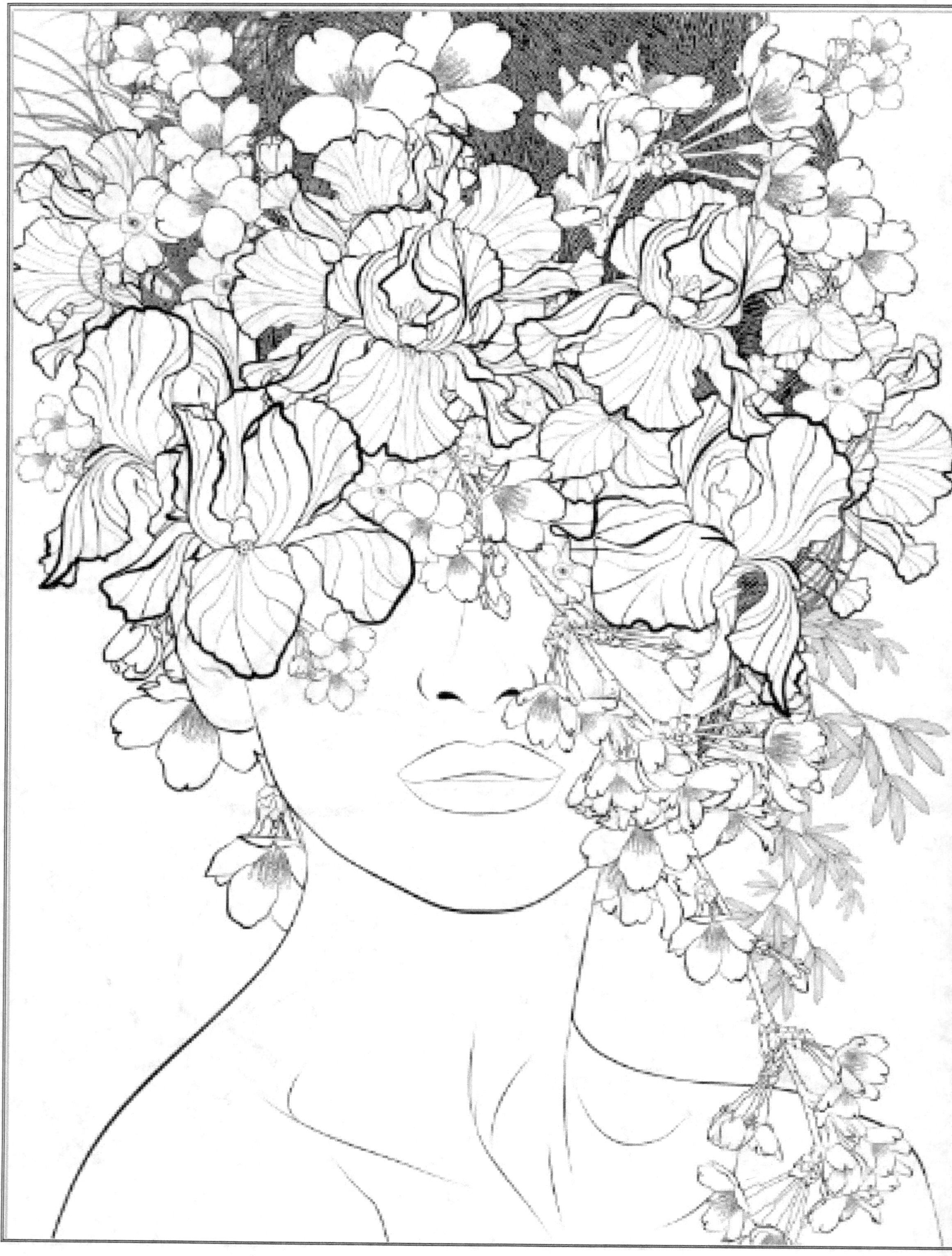

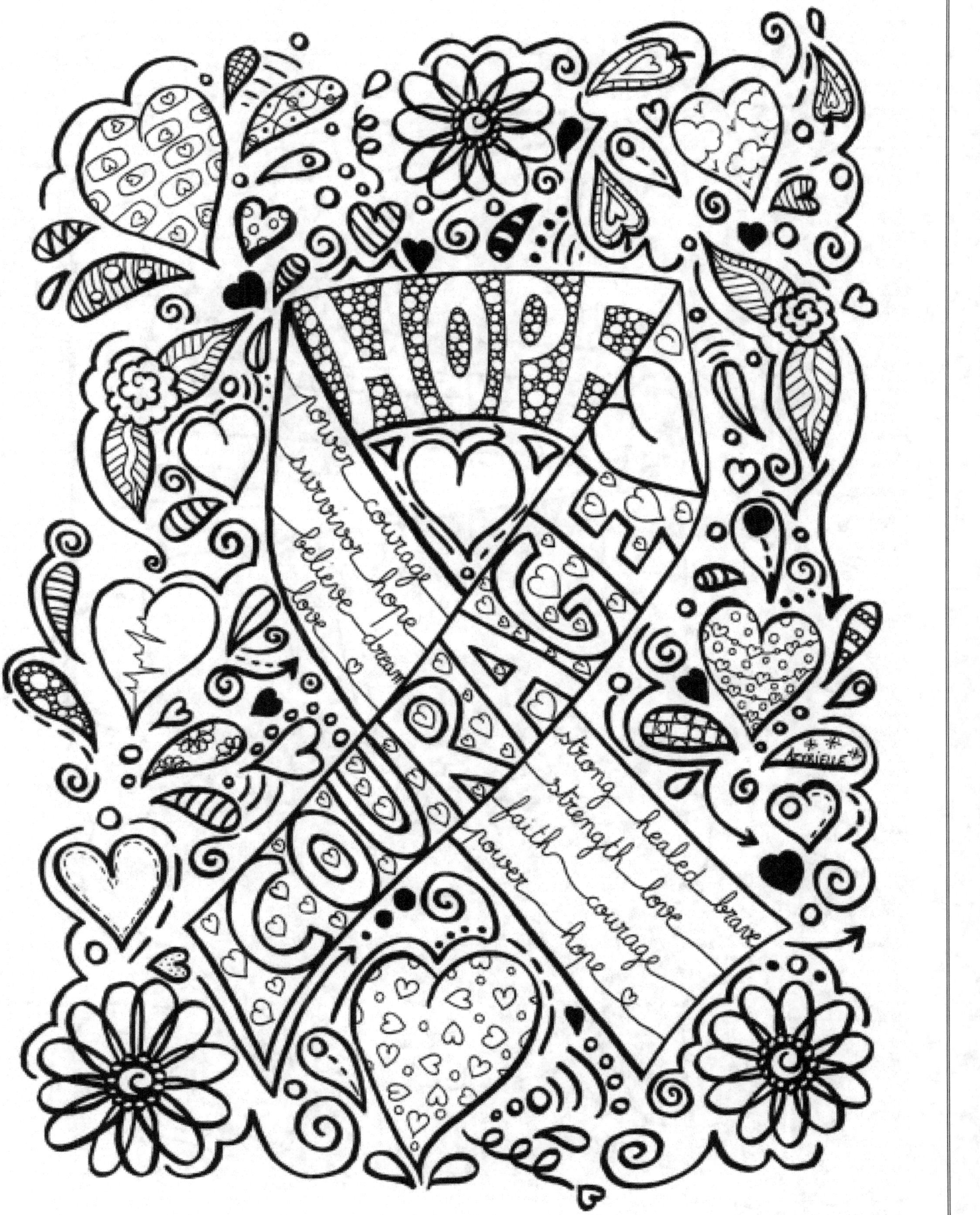
HOPE
COURAGE
power courage
survivor hope
believe hope
love dream
strong healed brave
strength love
faith courage
power hope

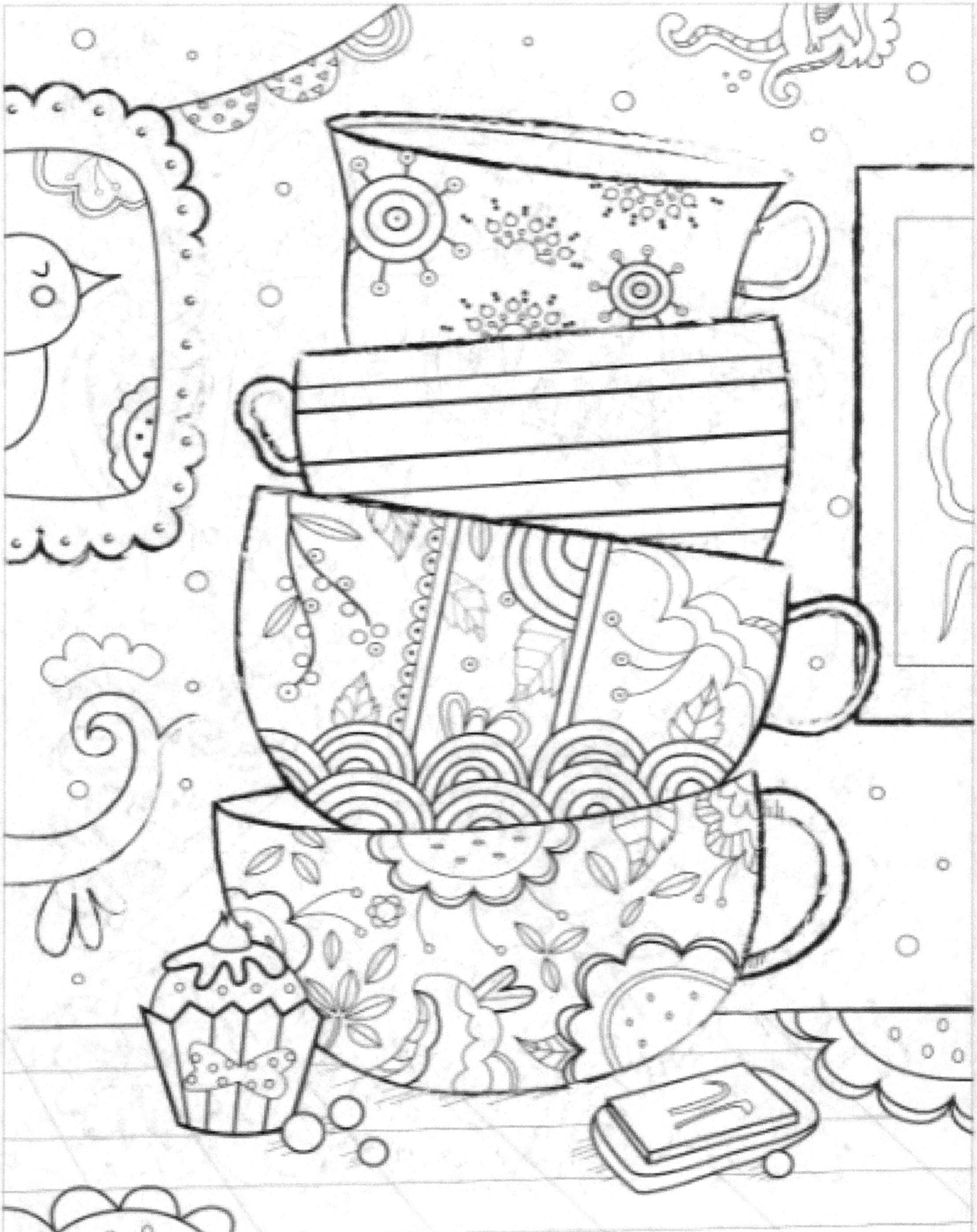

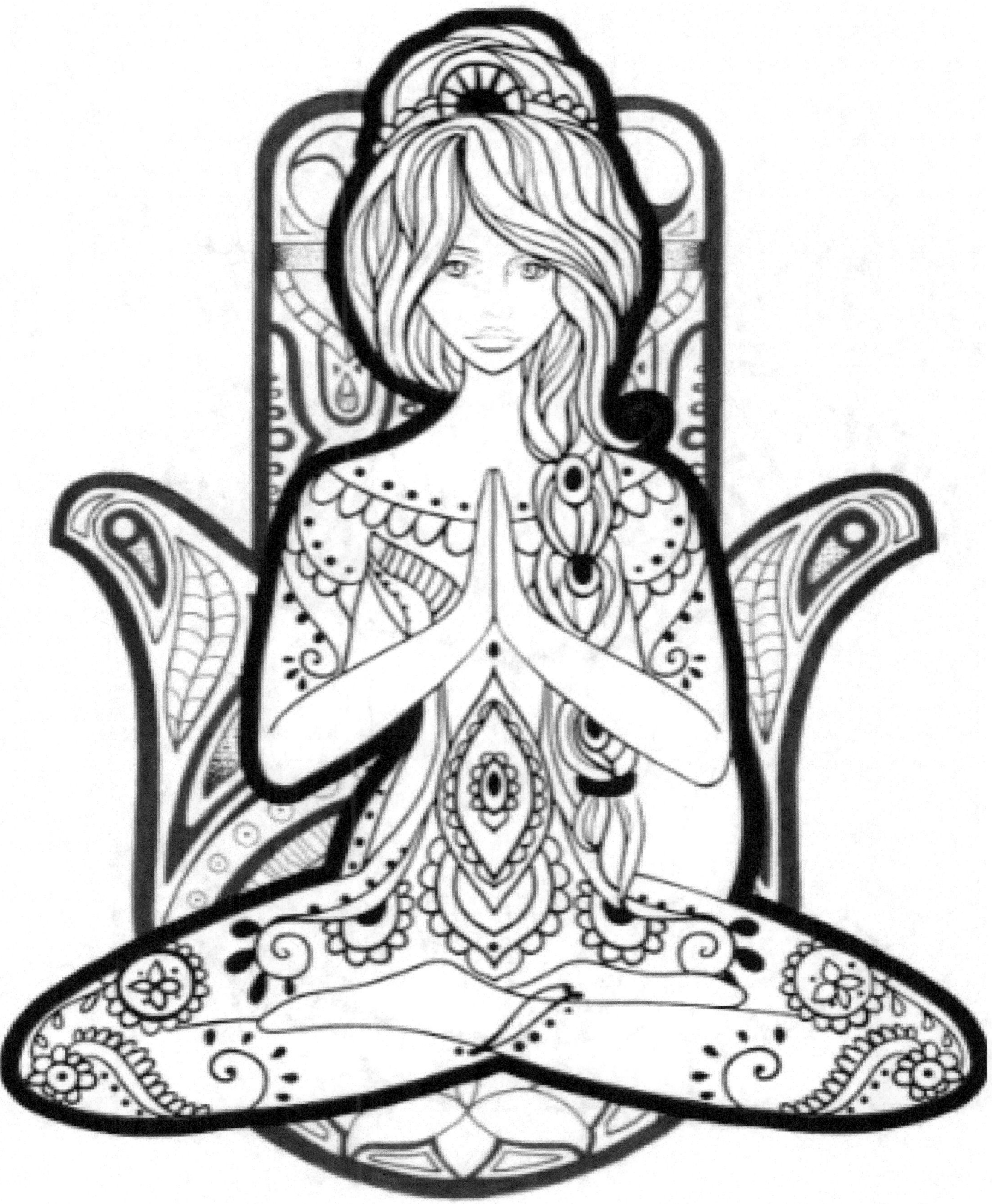

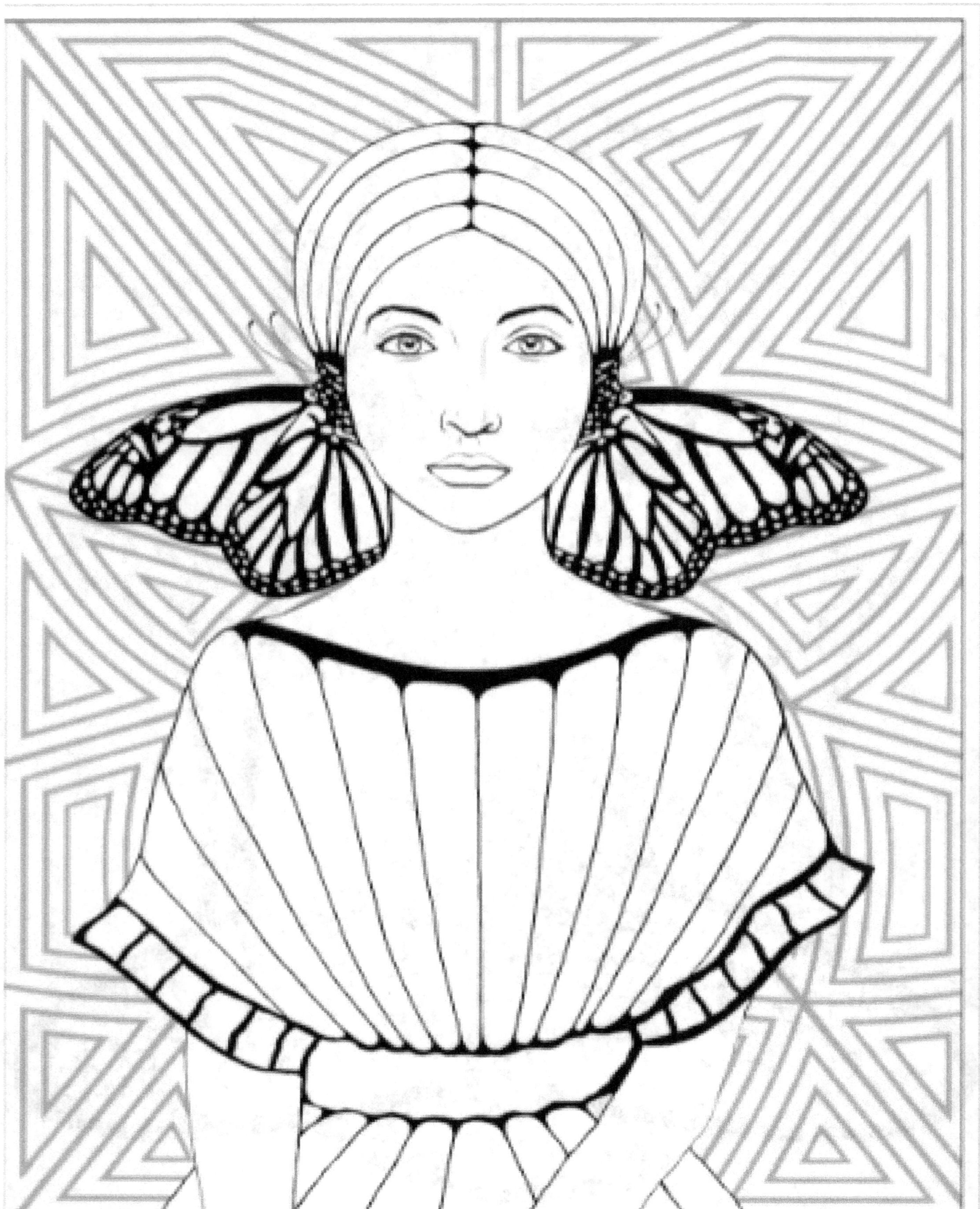

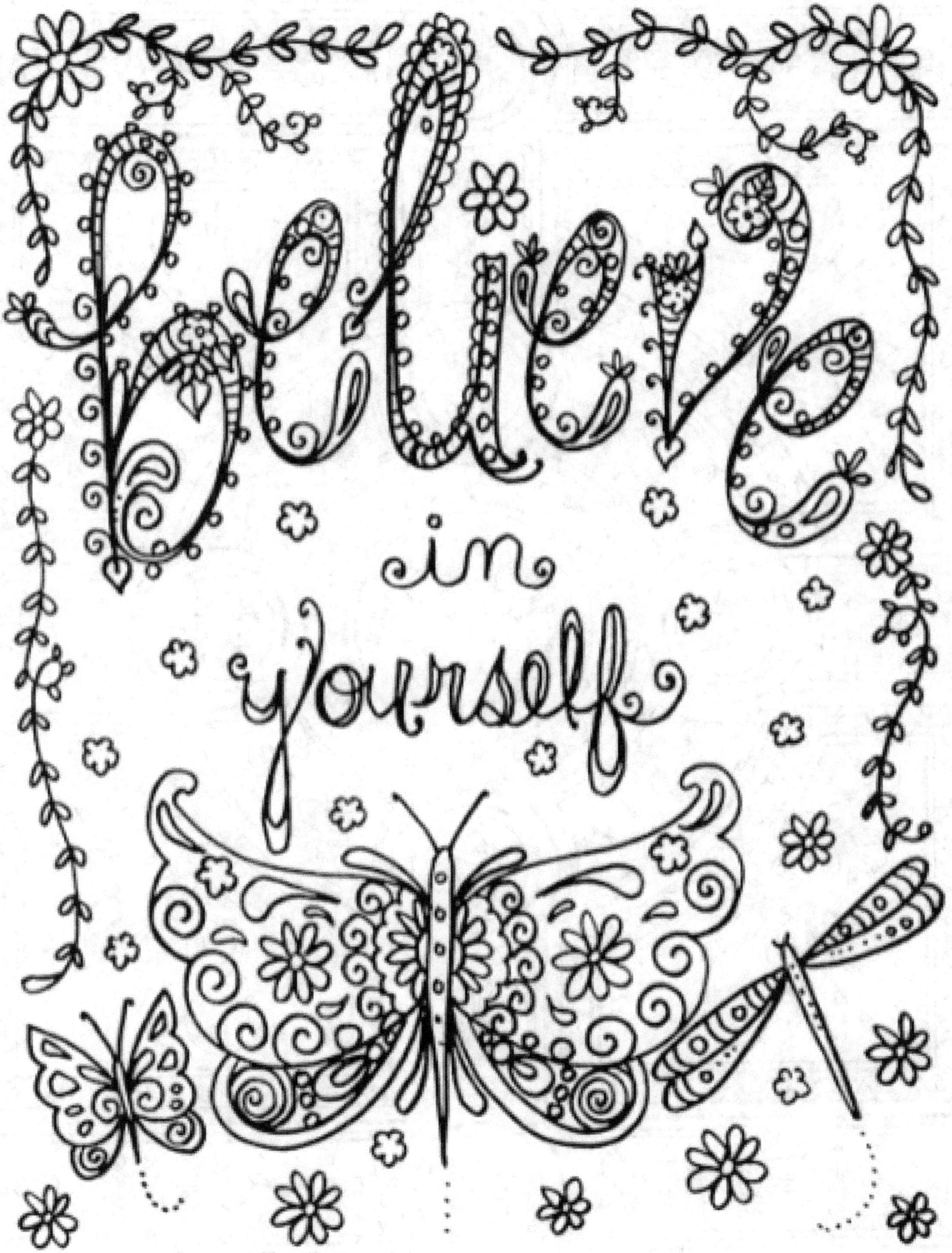
believe
in
yourself

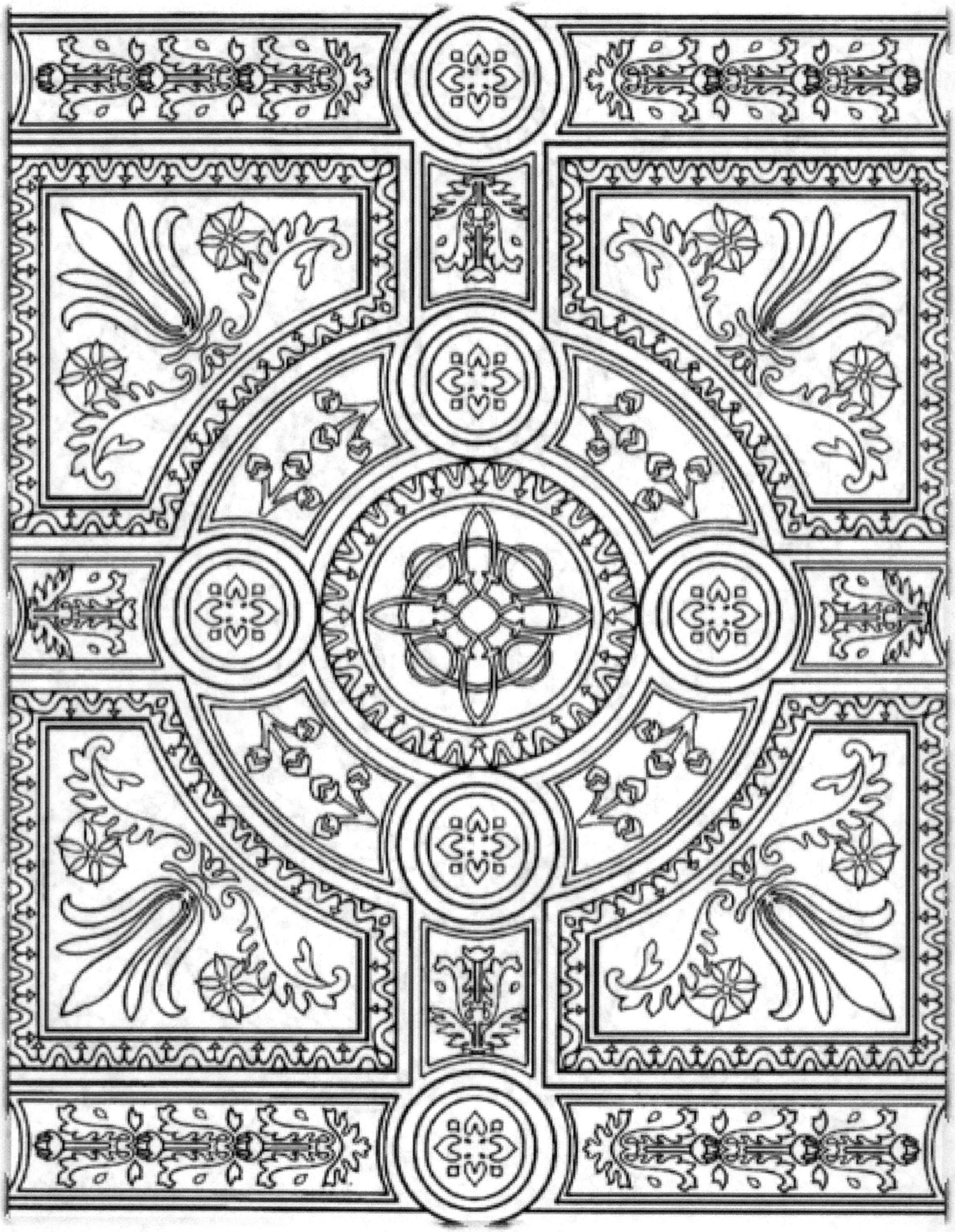

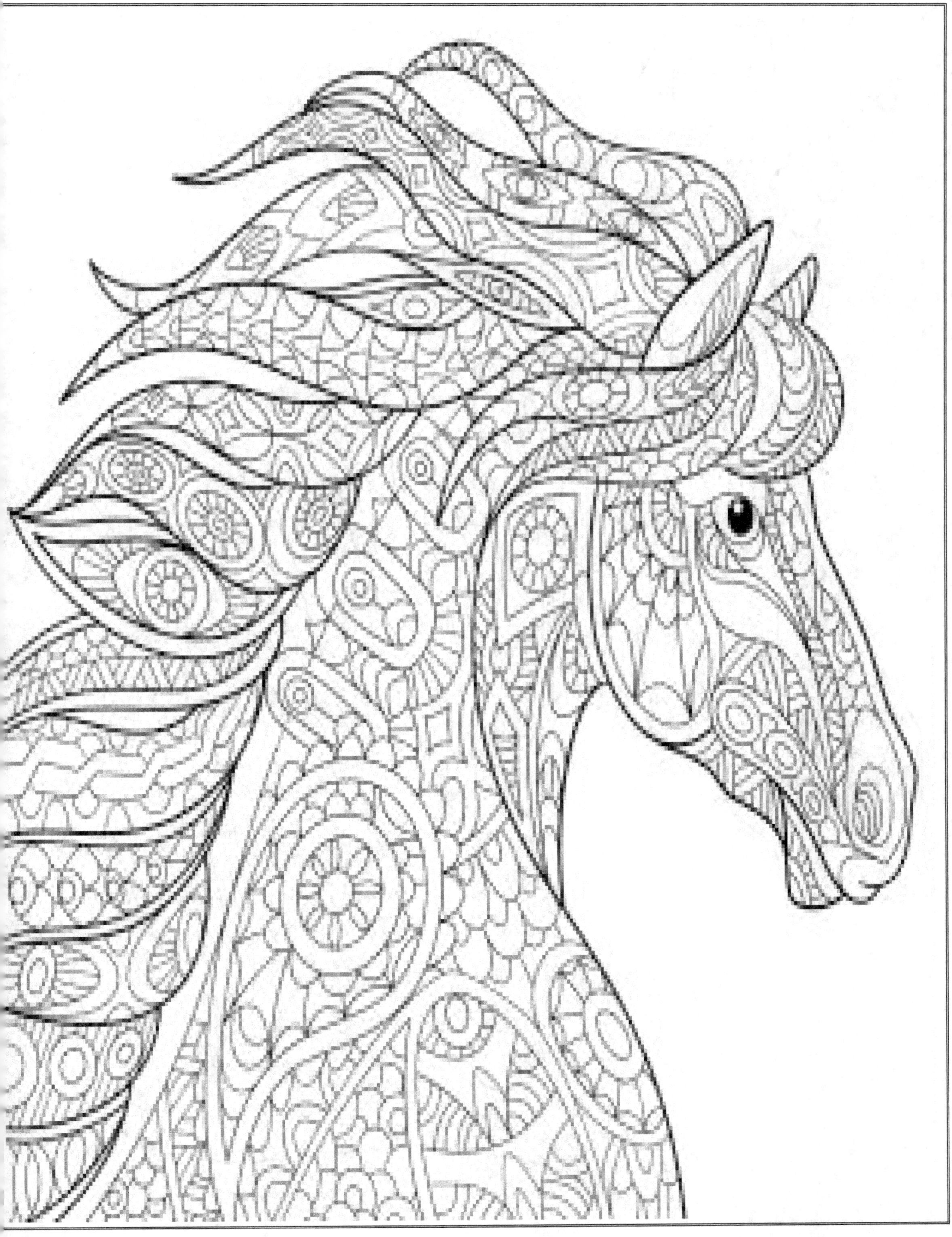

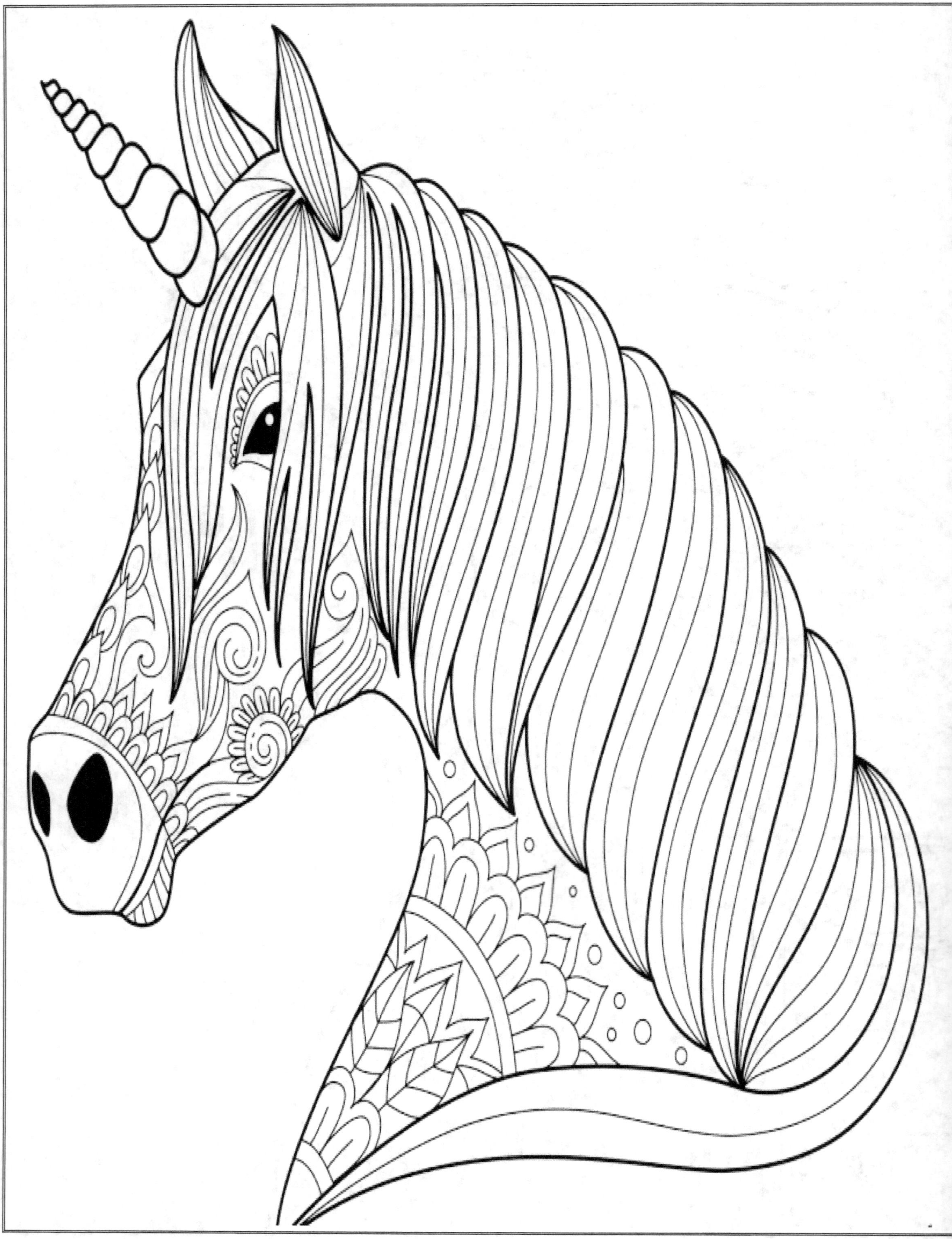

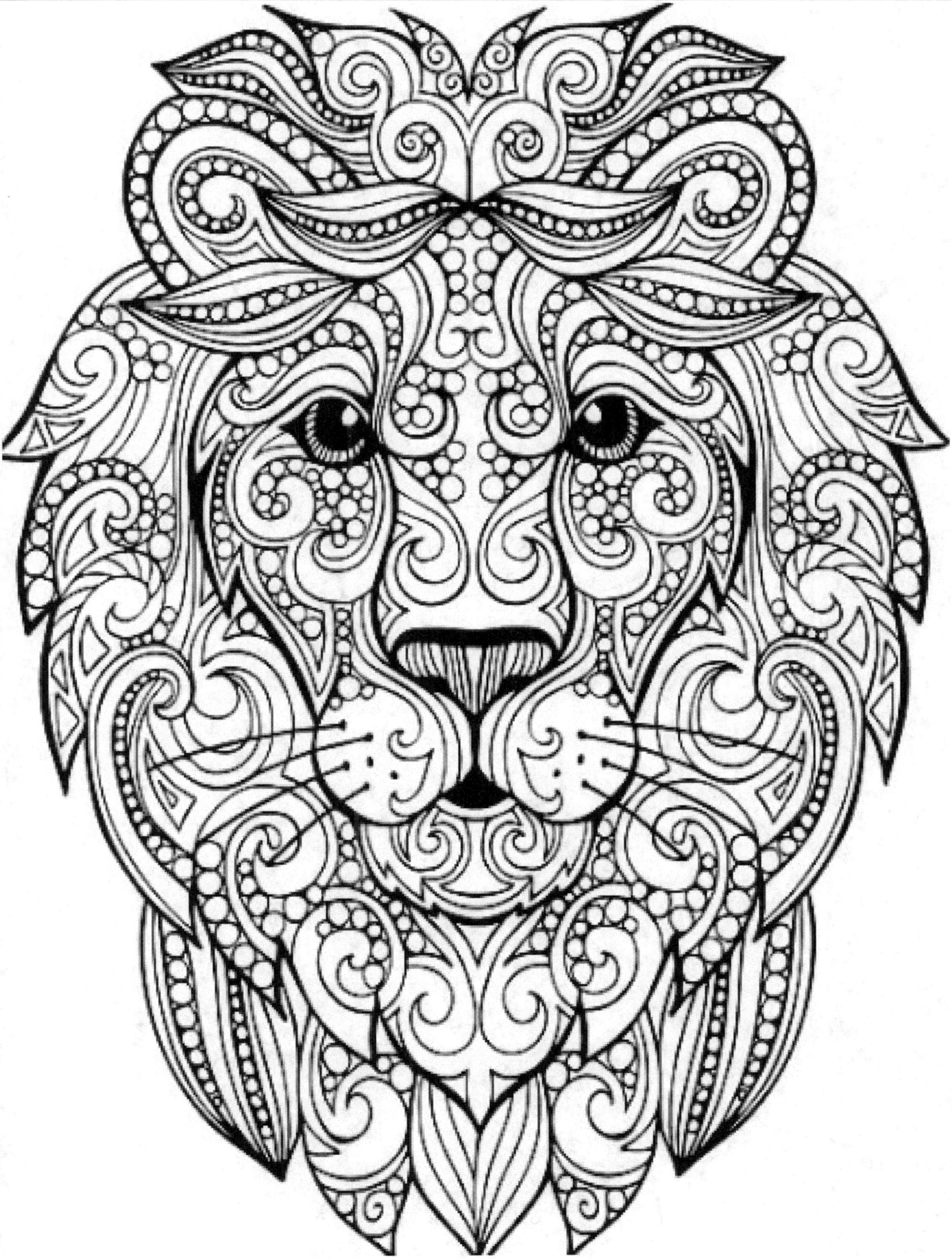

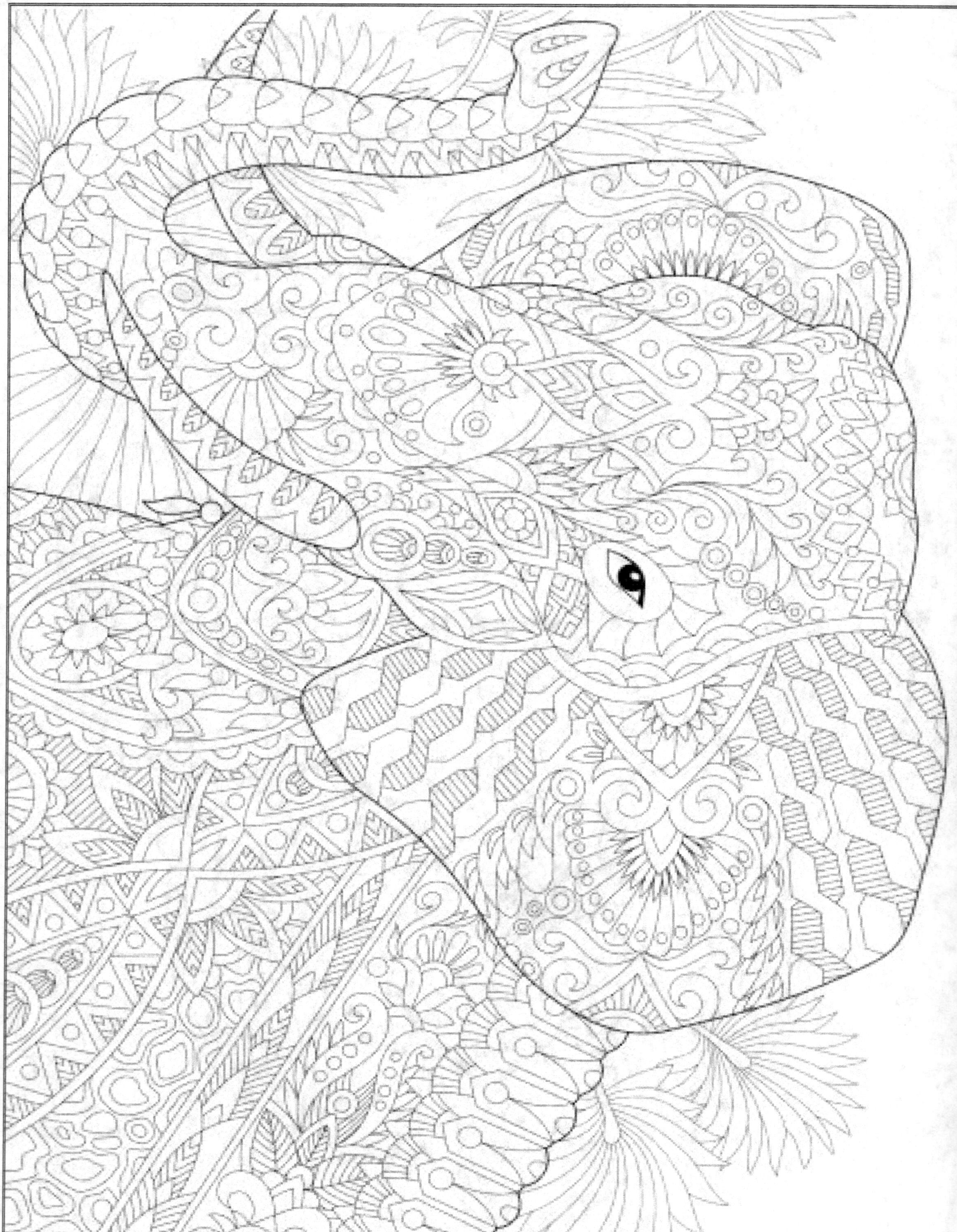

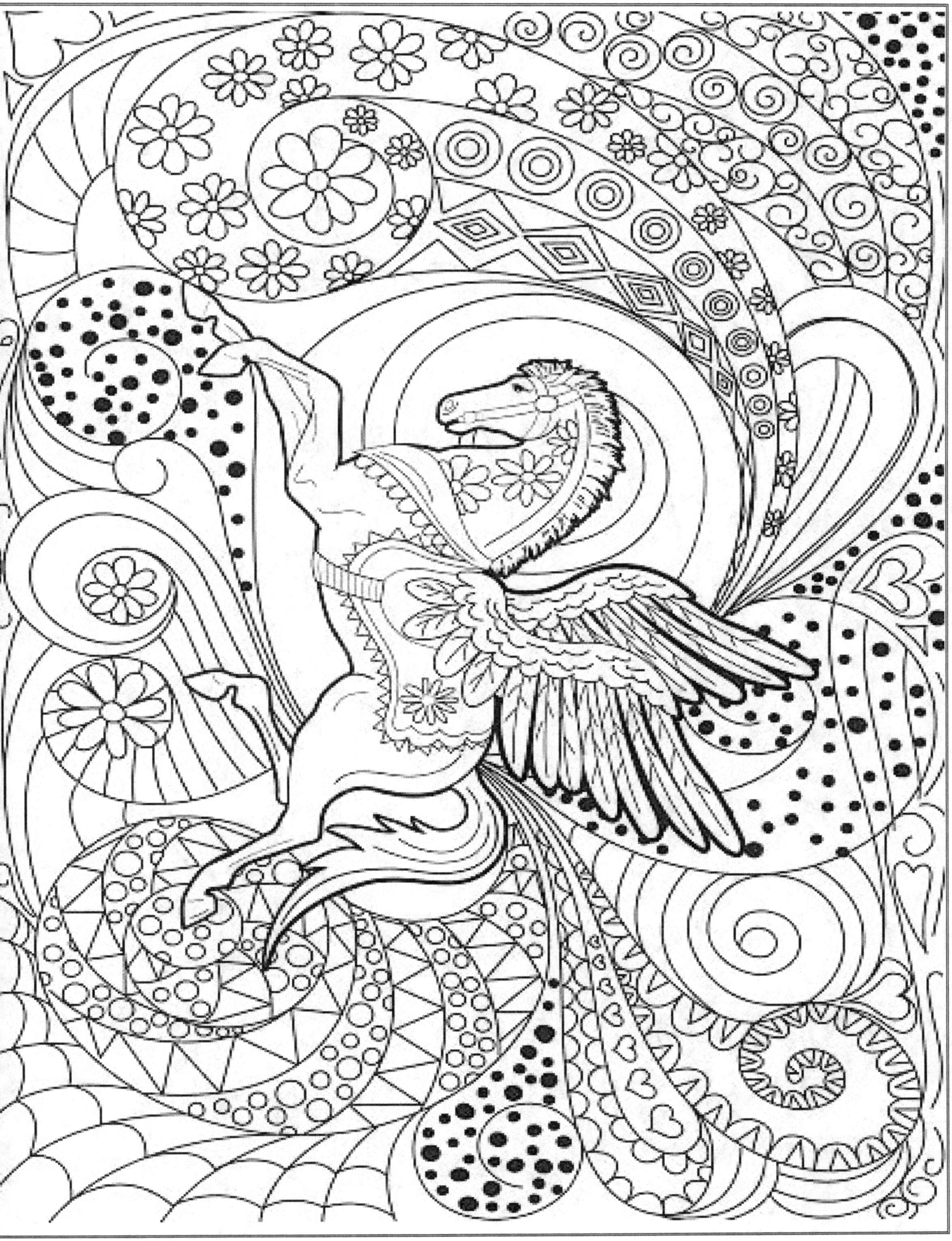

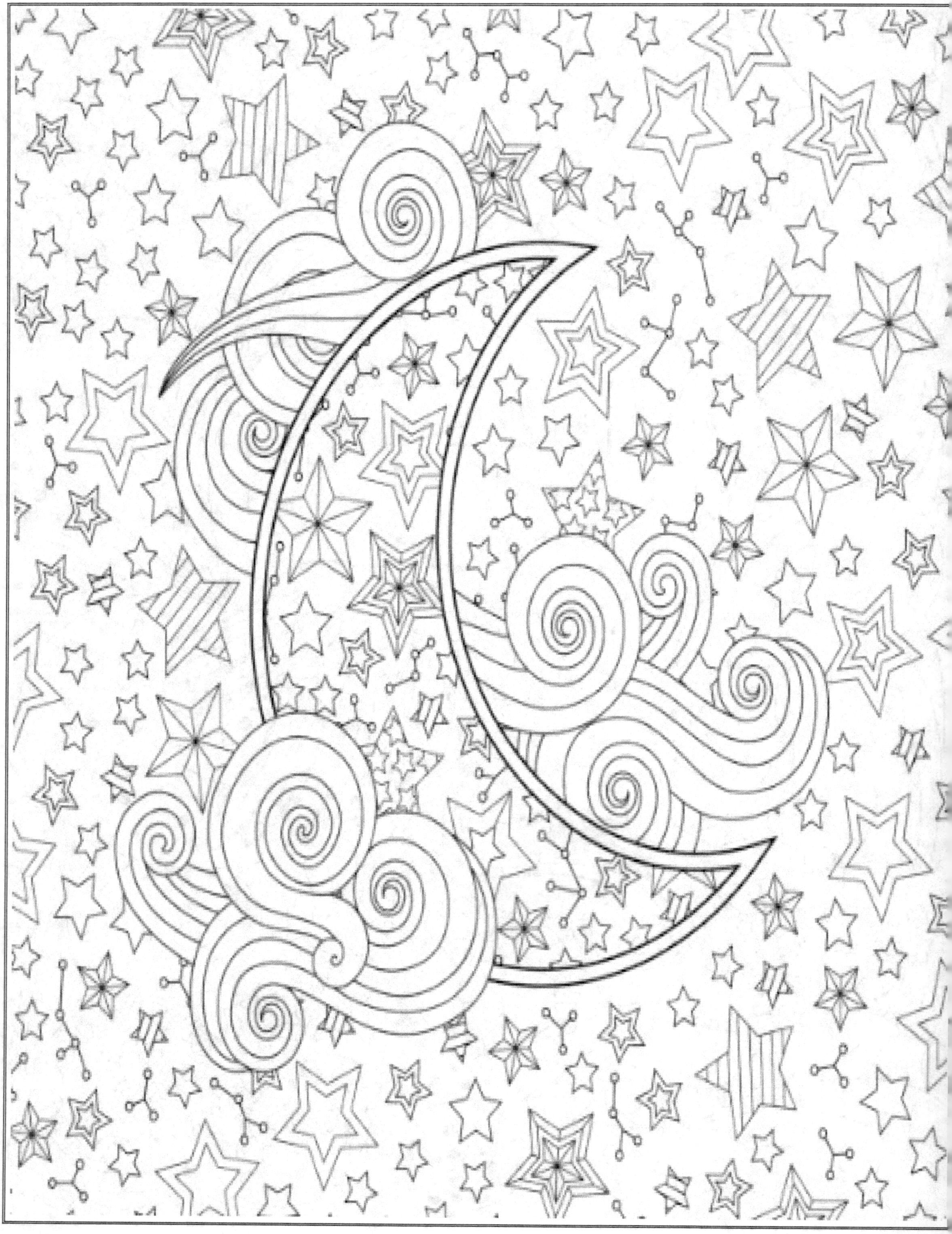

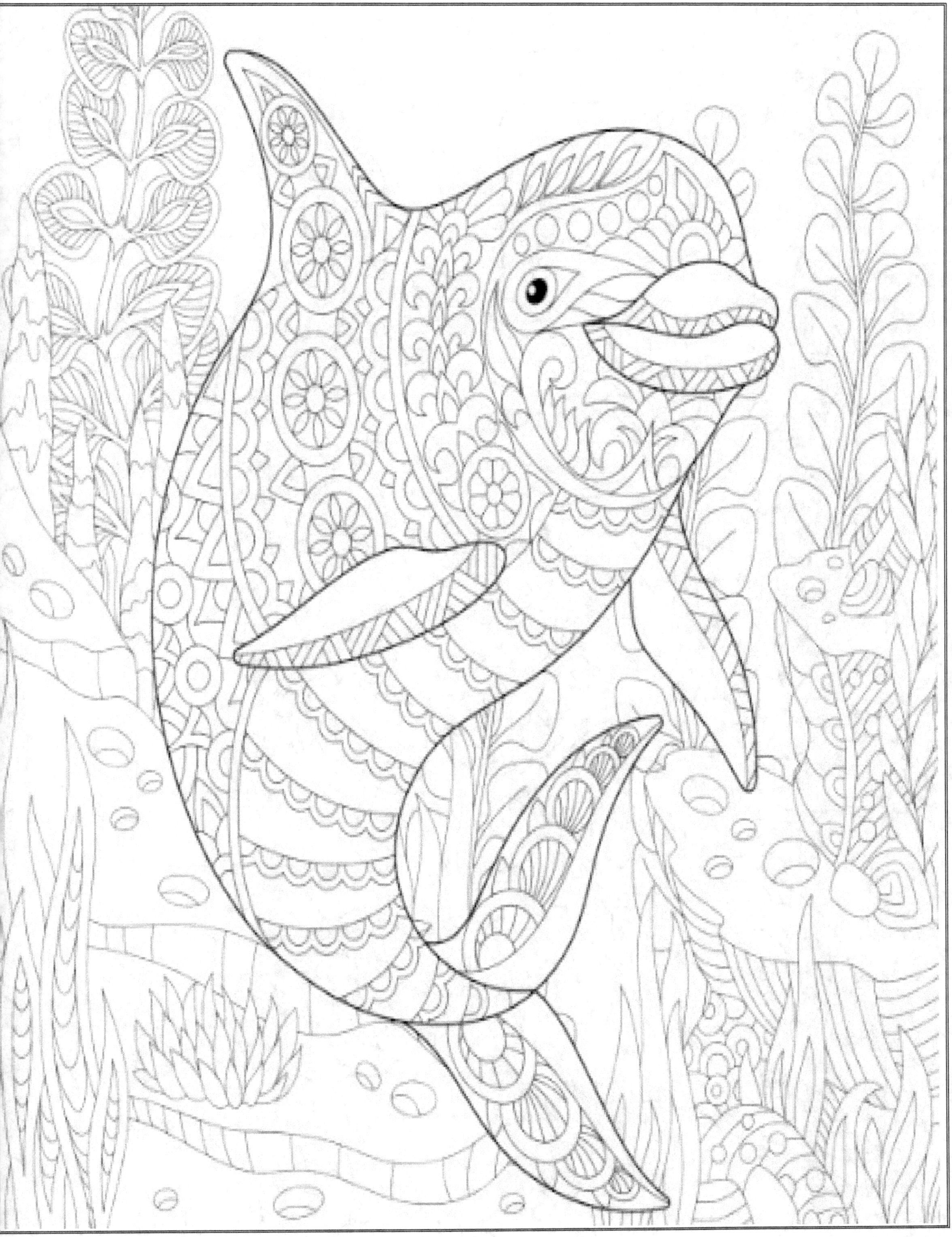

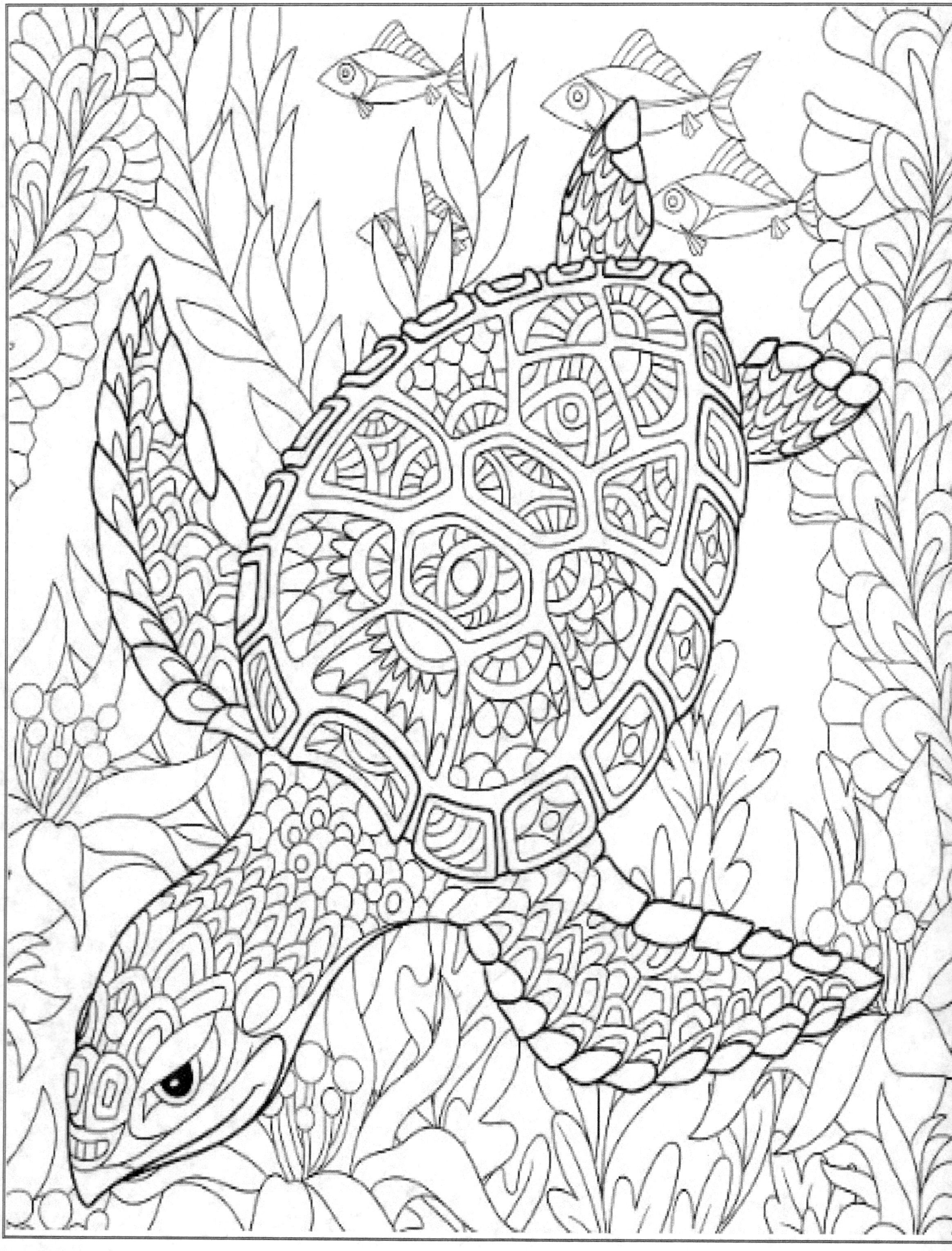

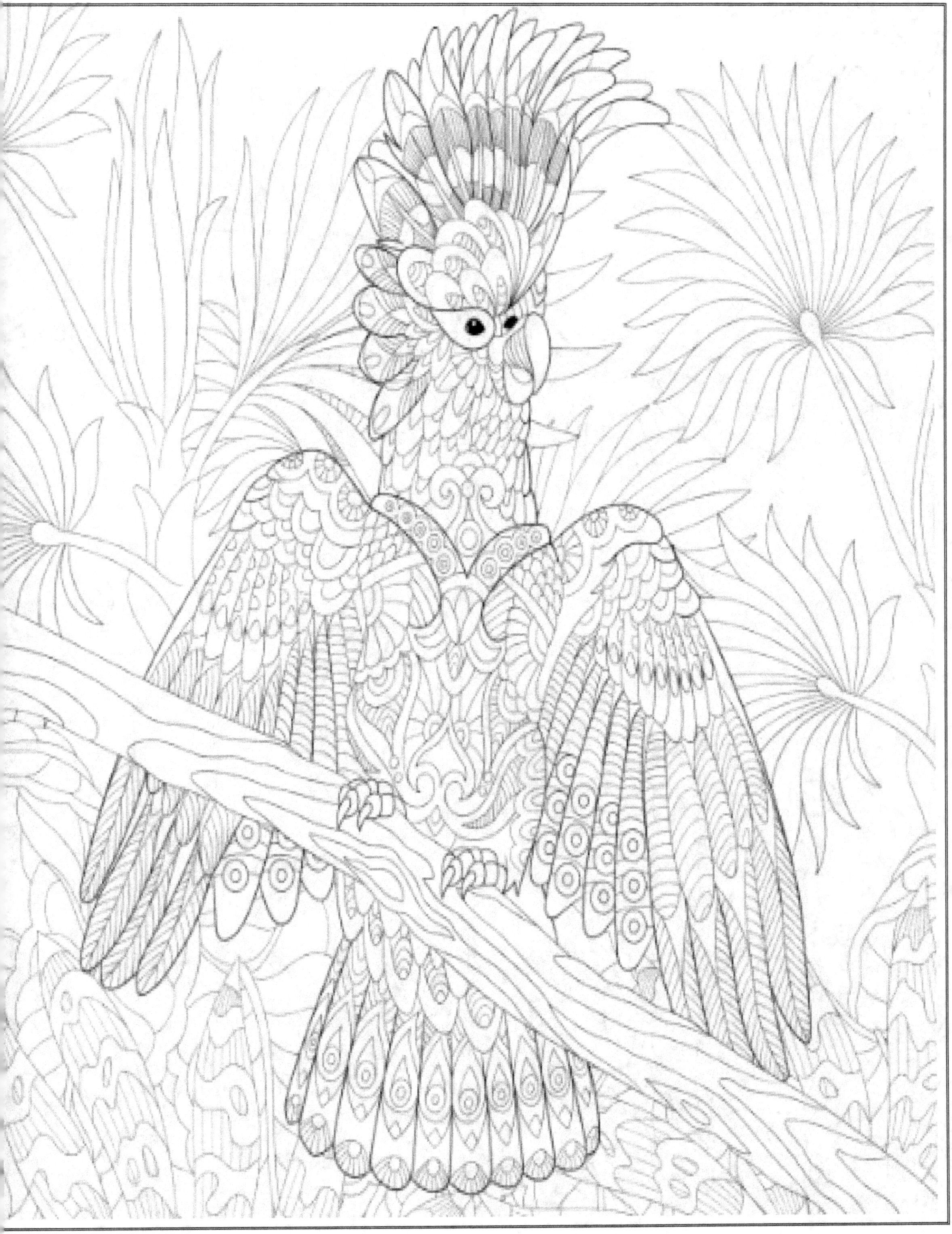

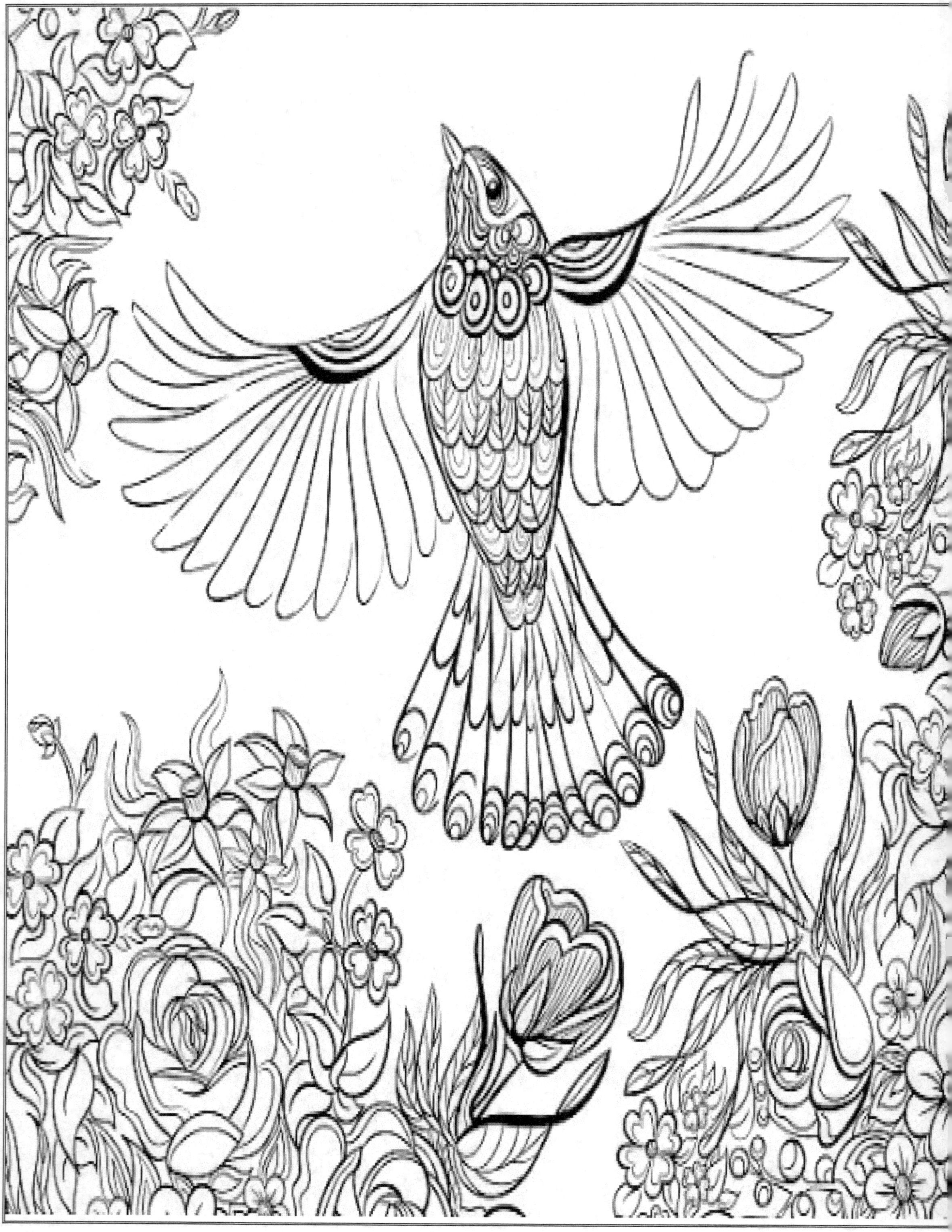

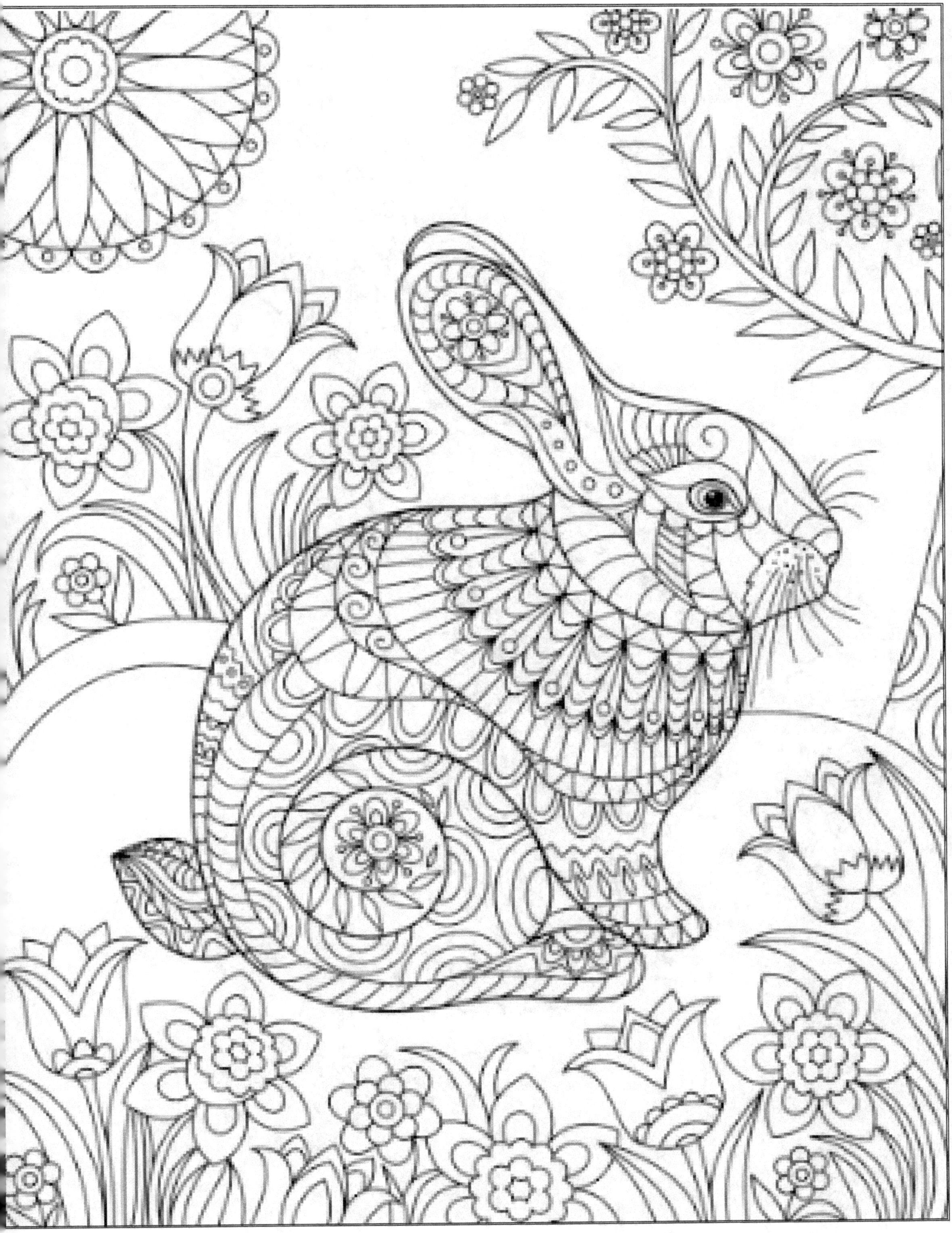

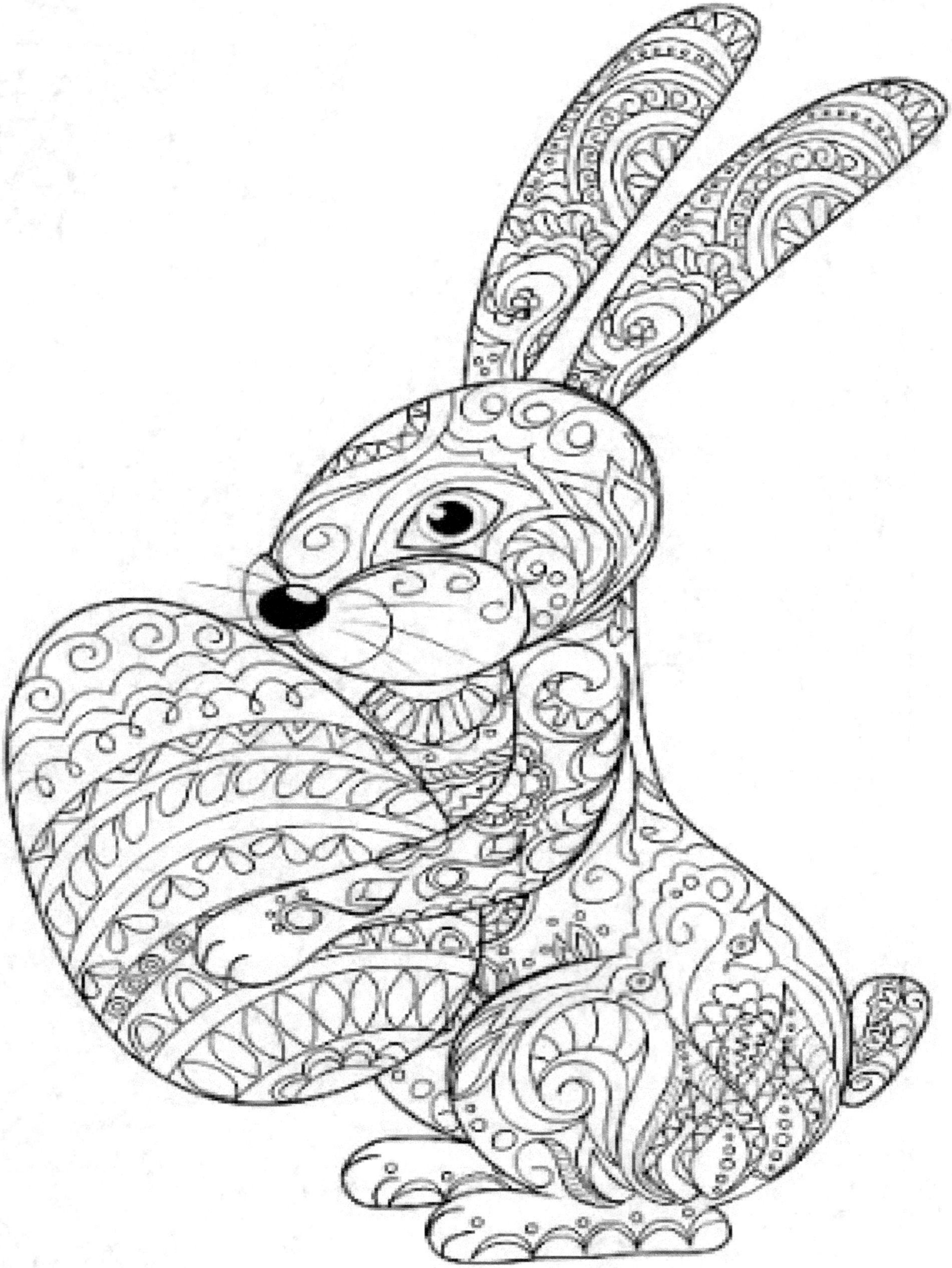

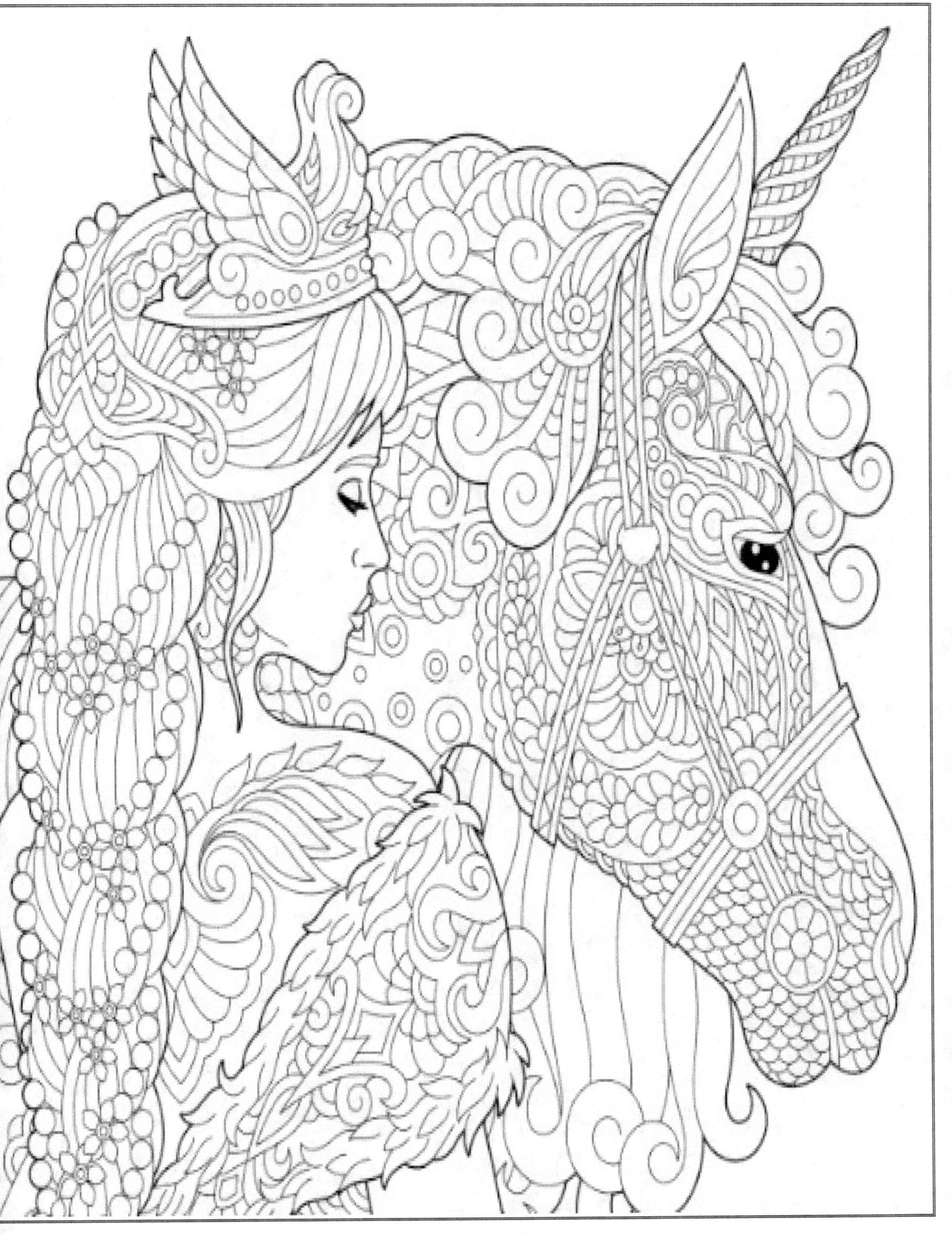

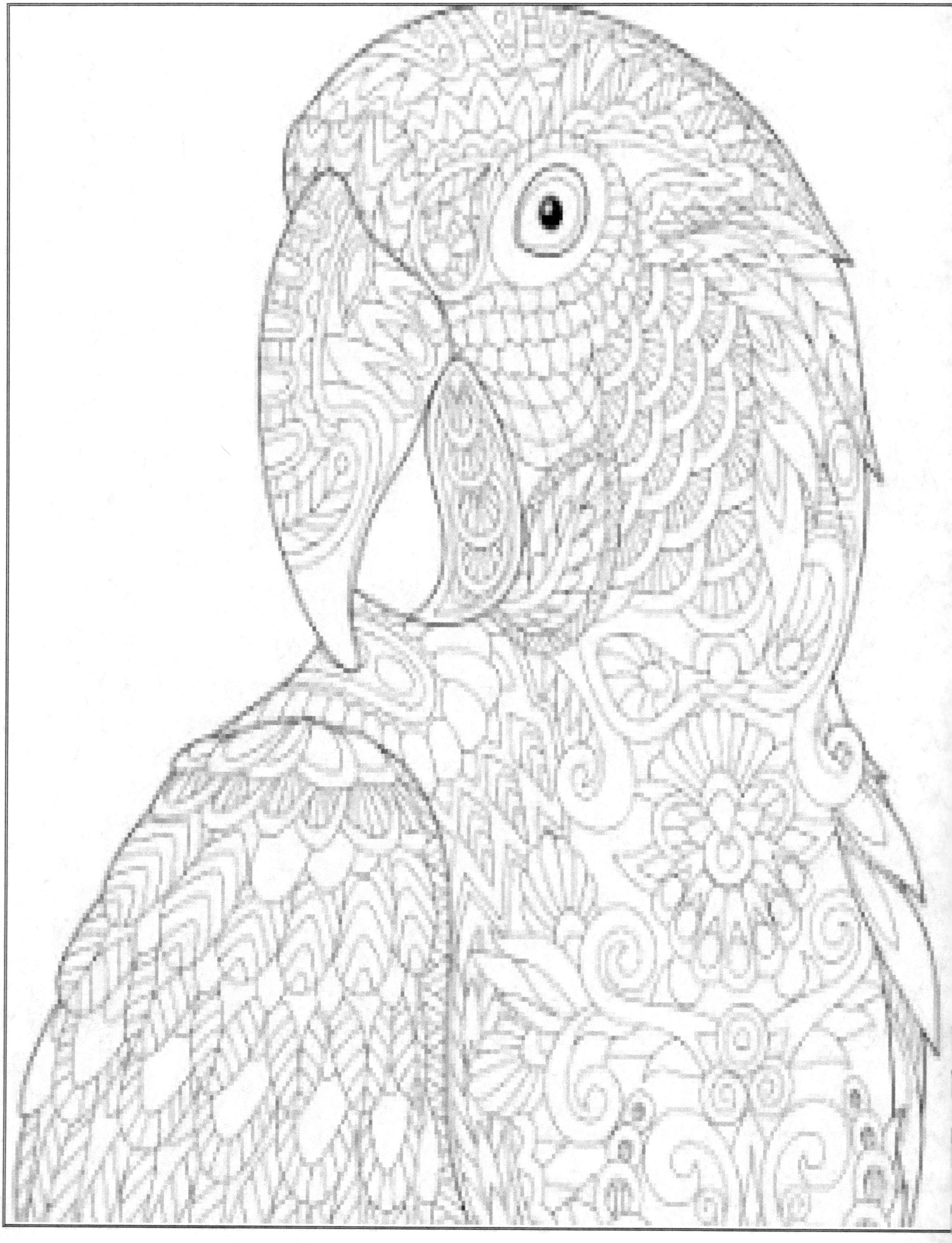

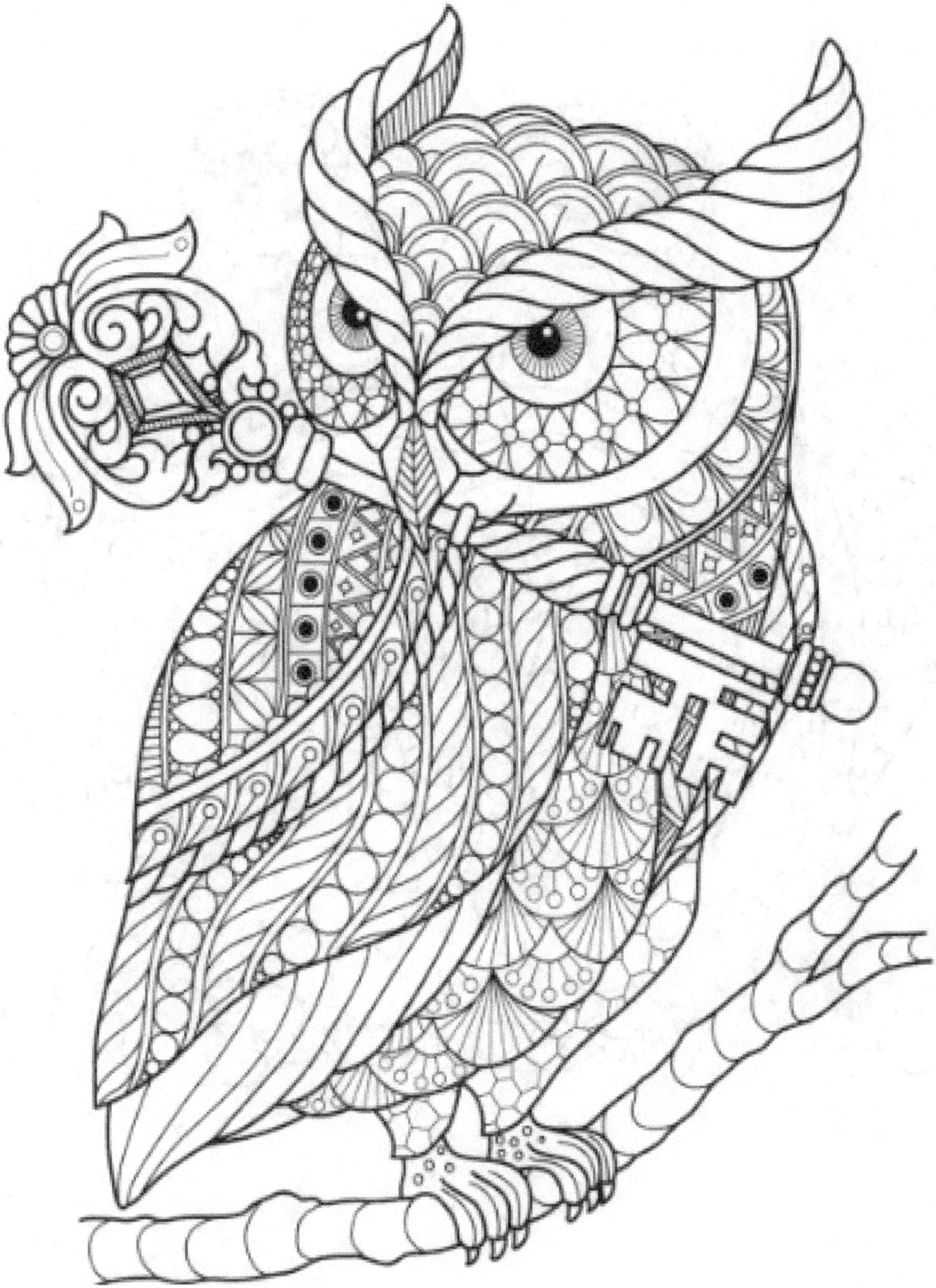

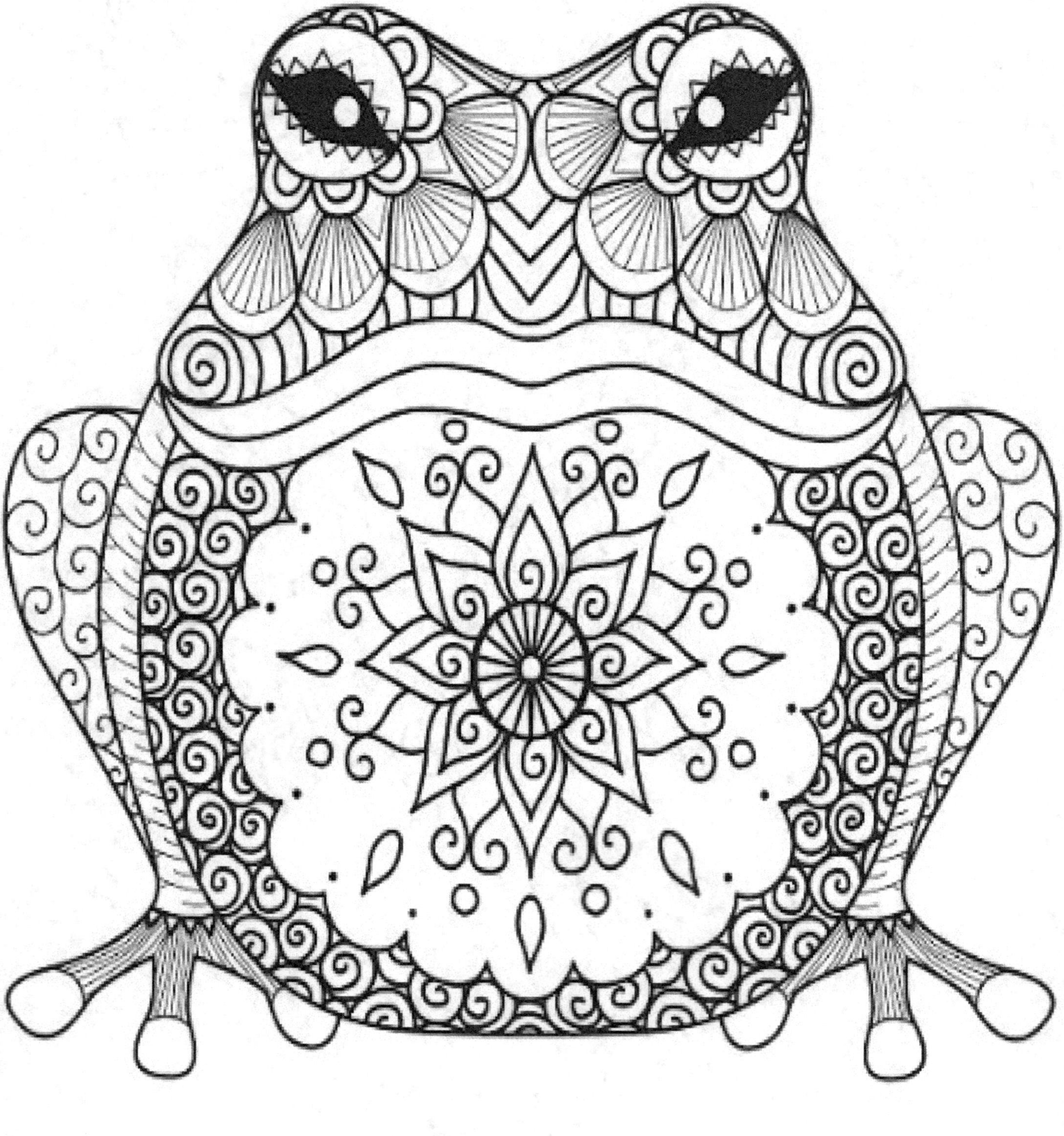

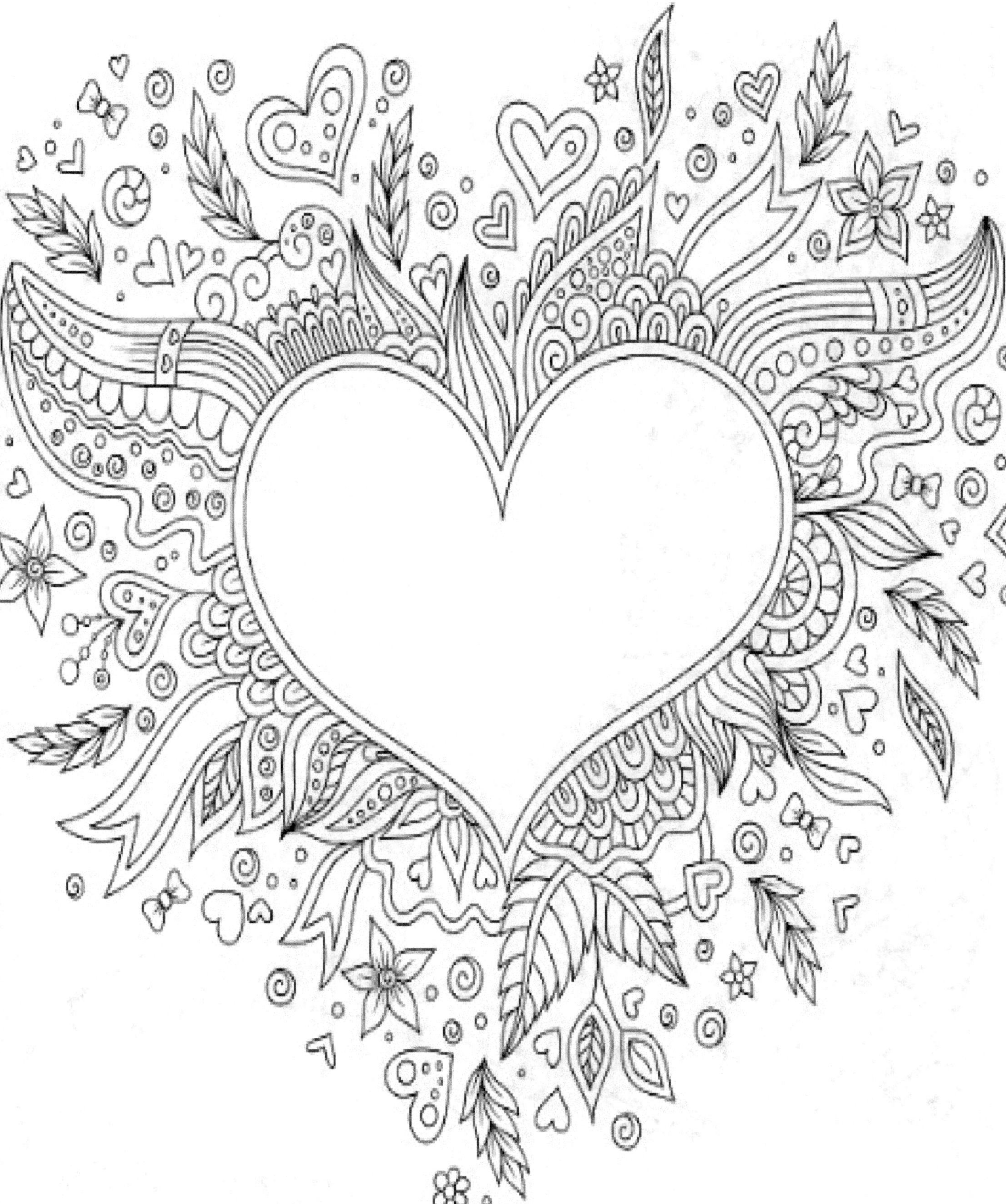

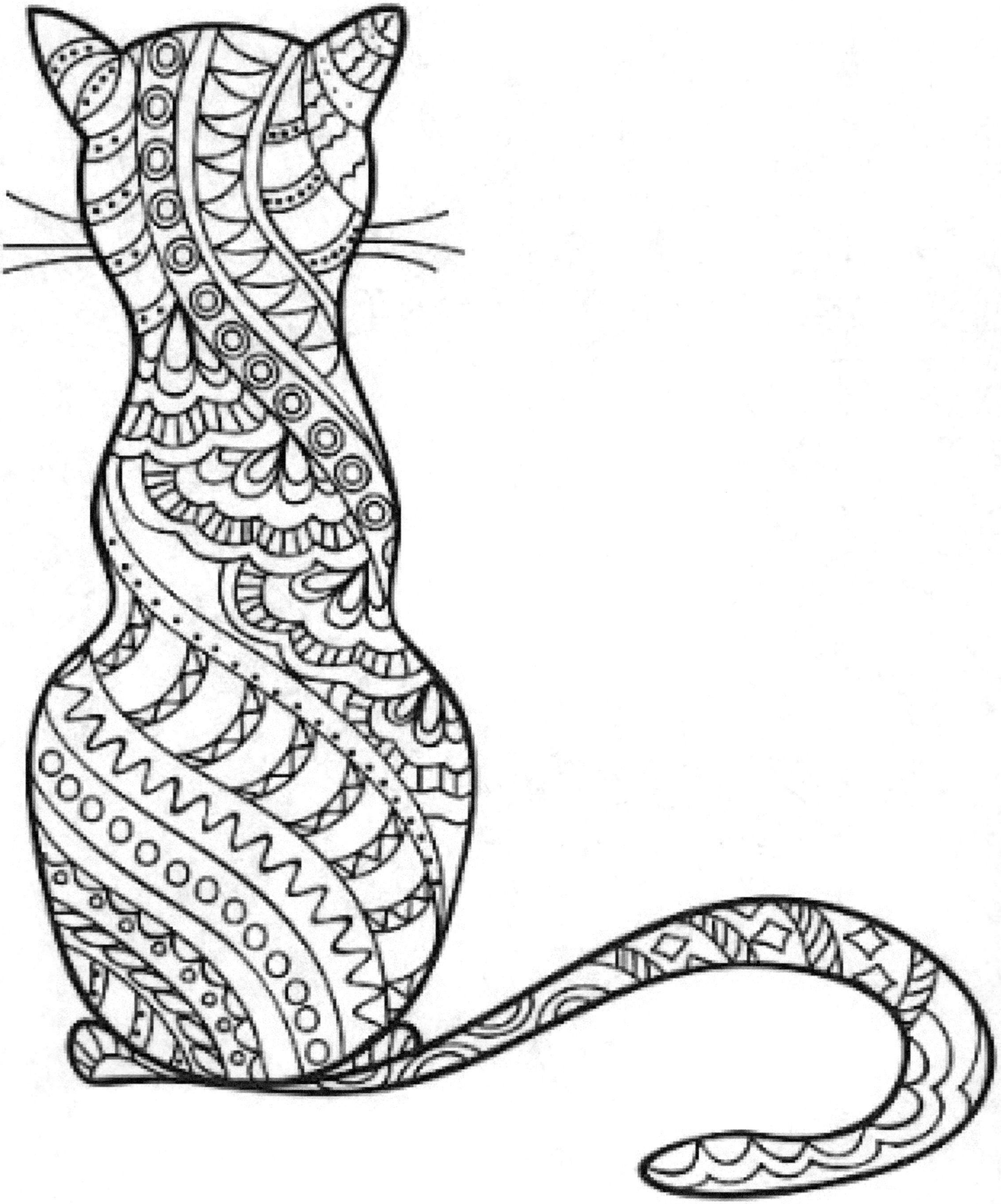

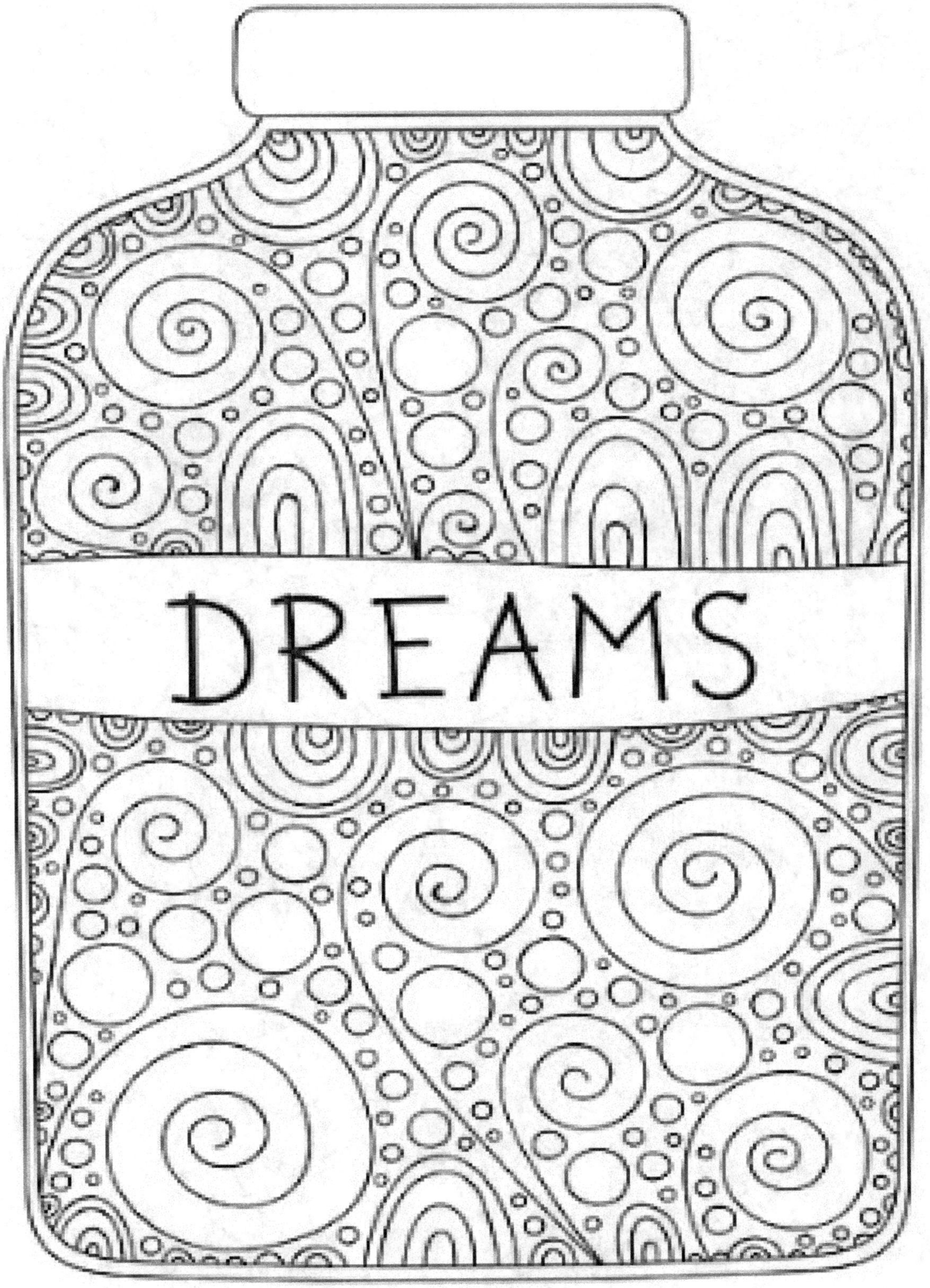
DREAMS

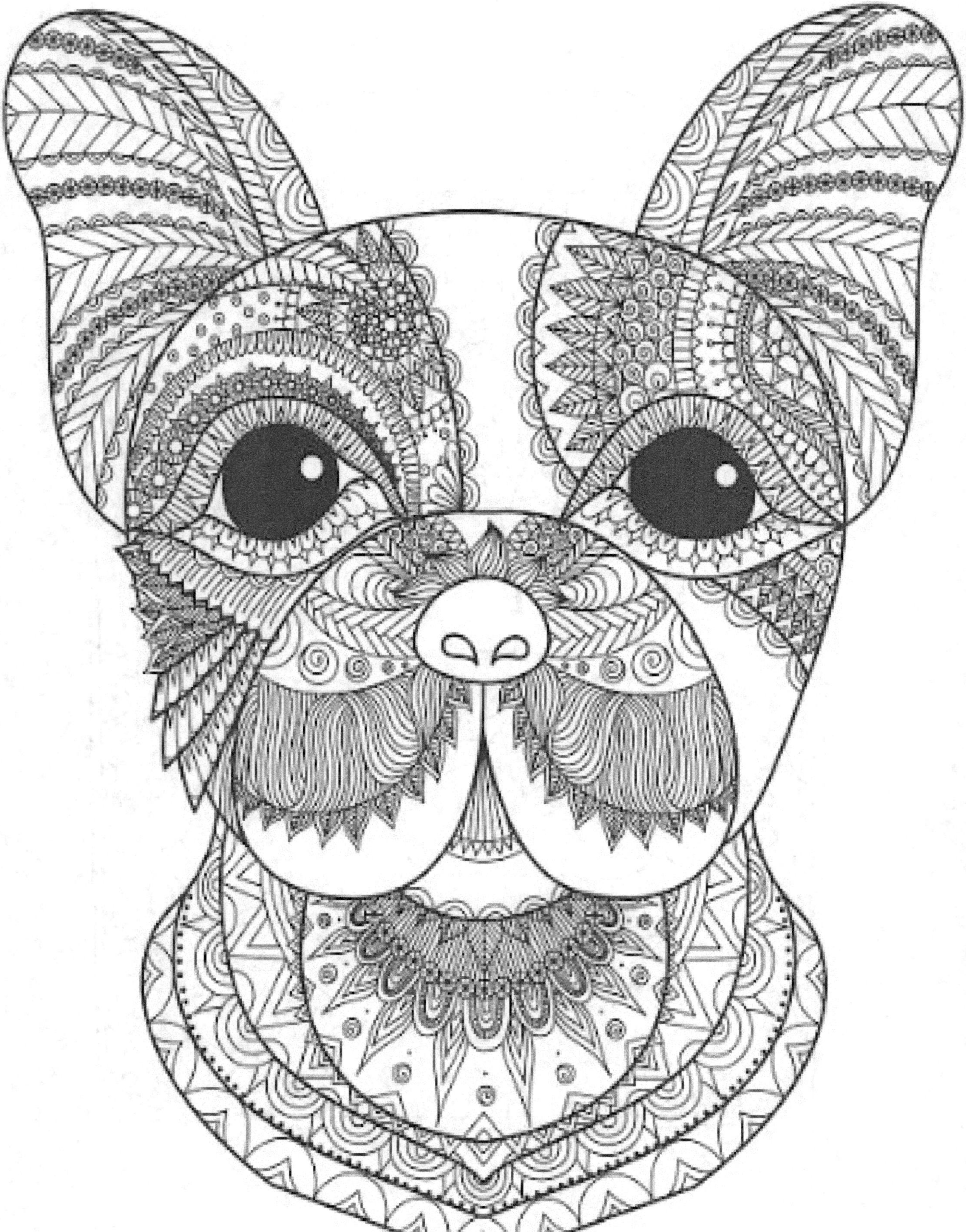

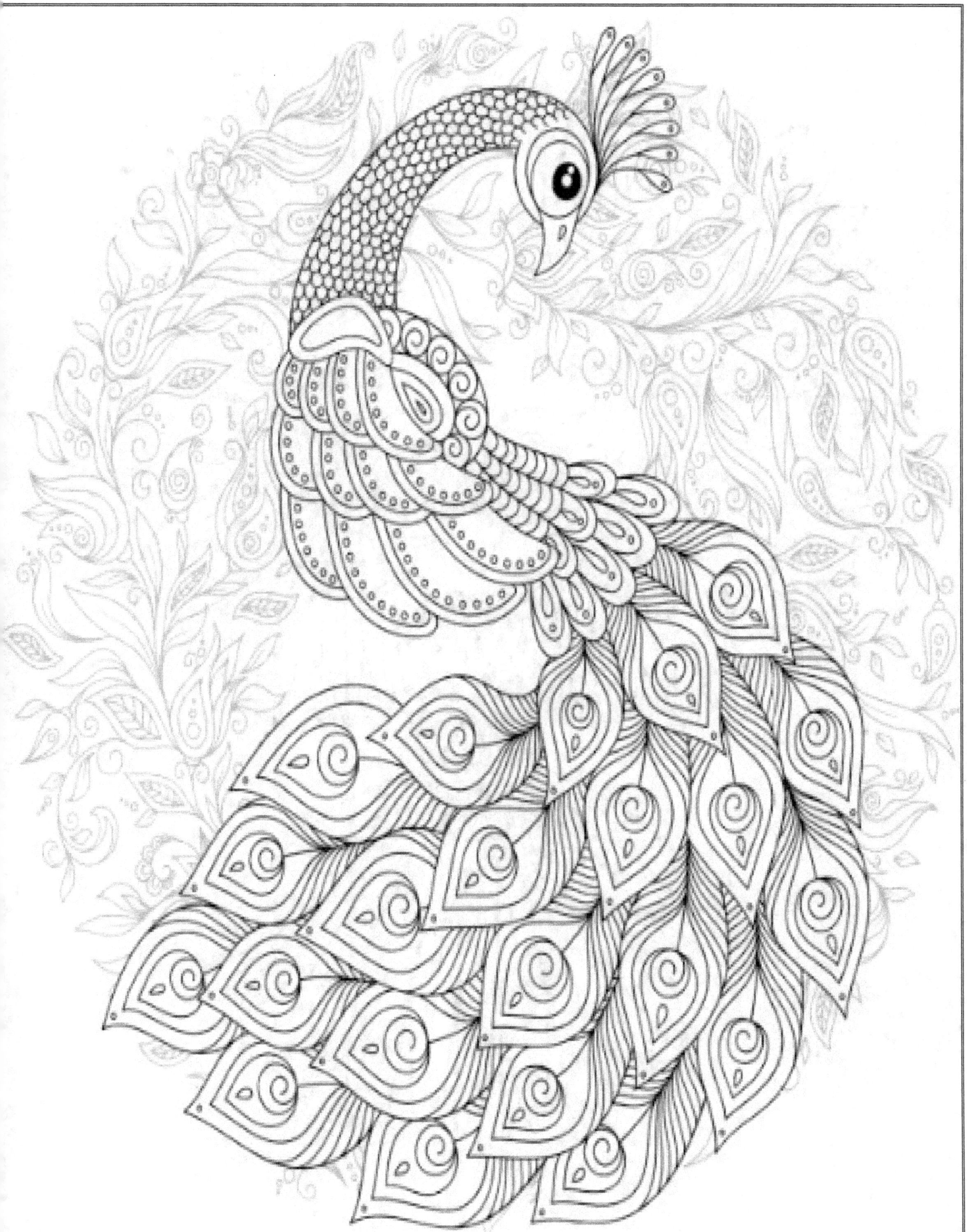

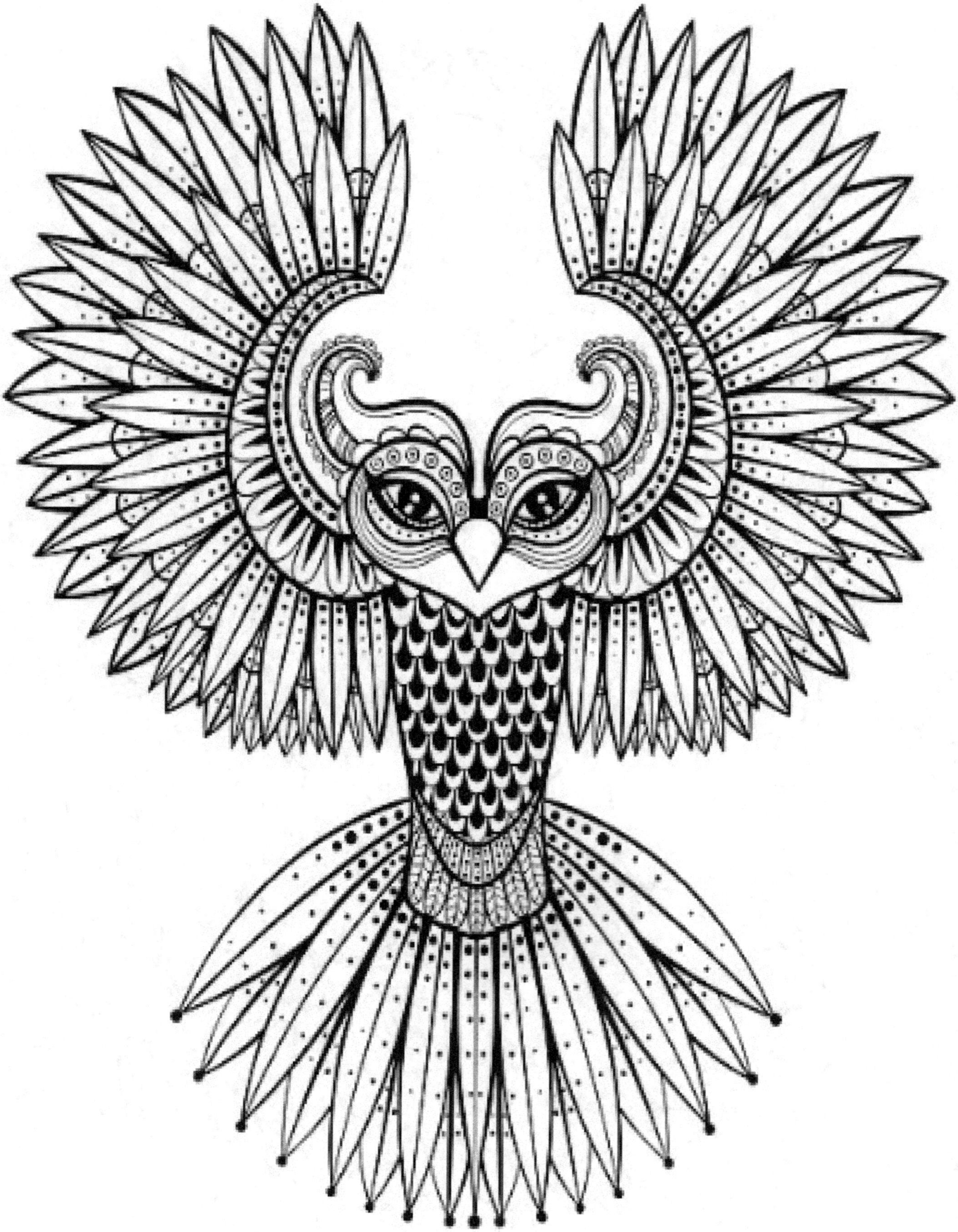

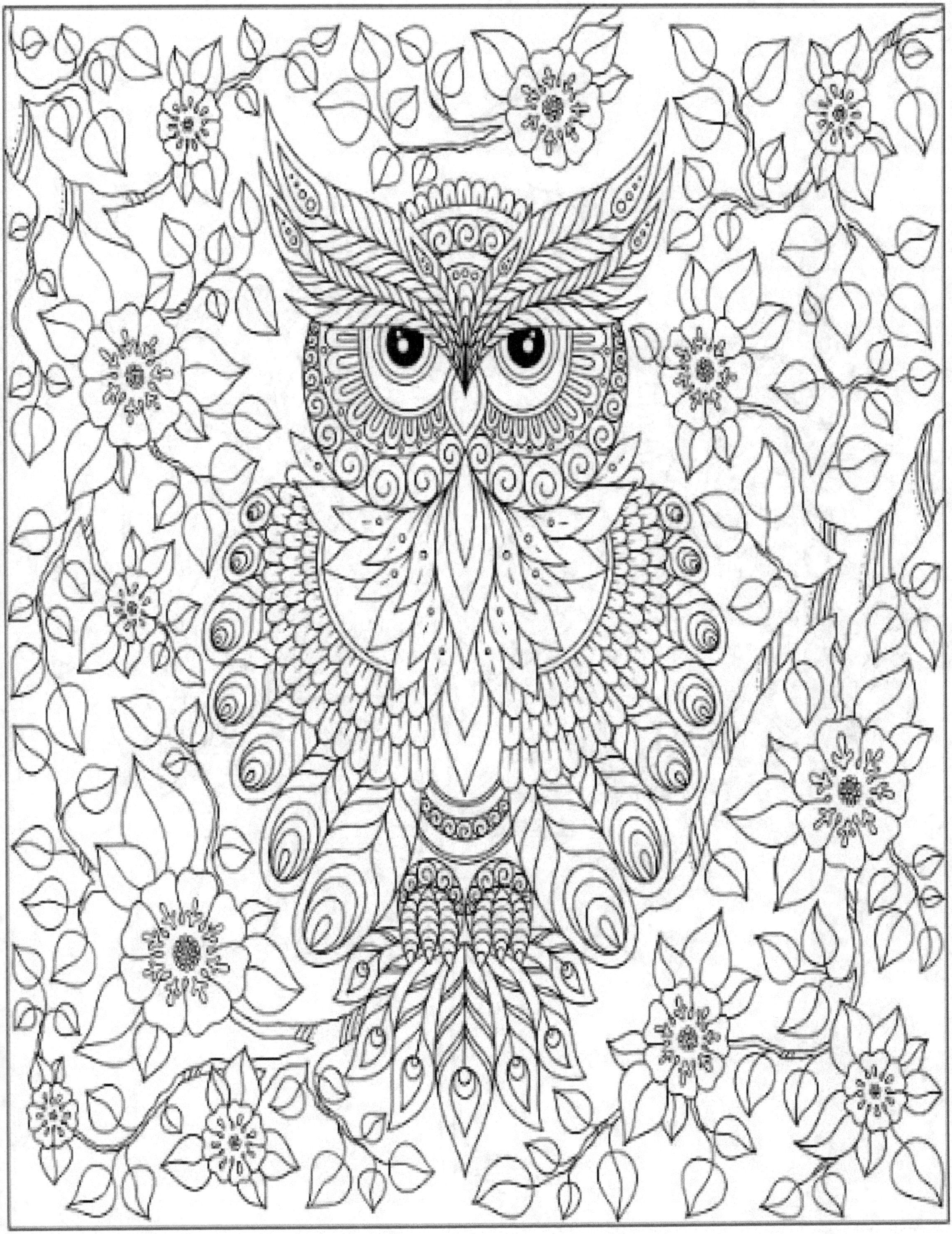

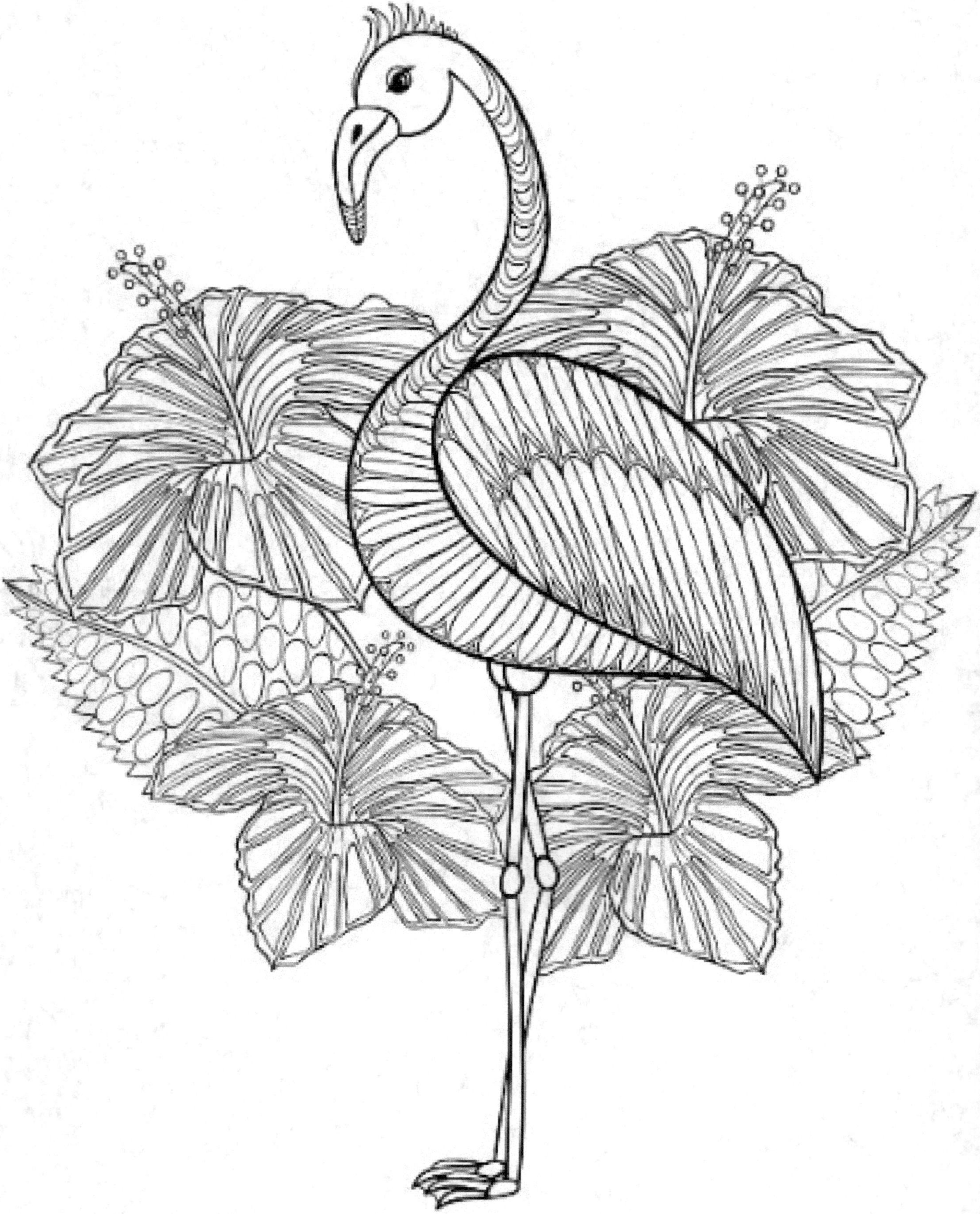

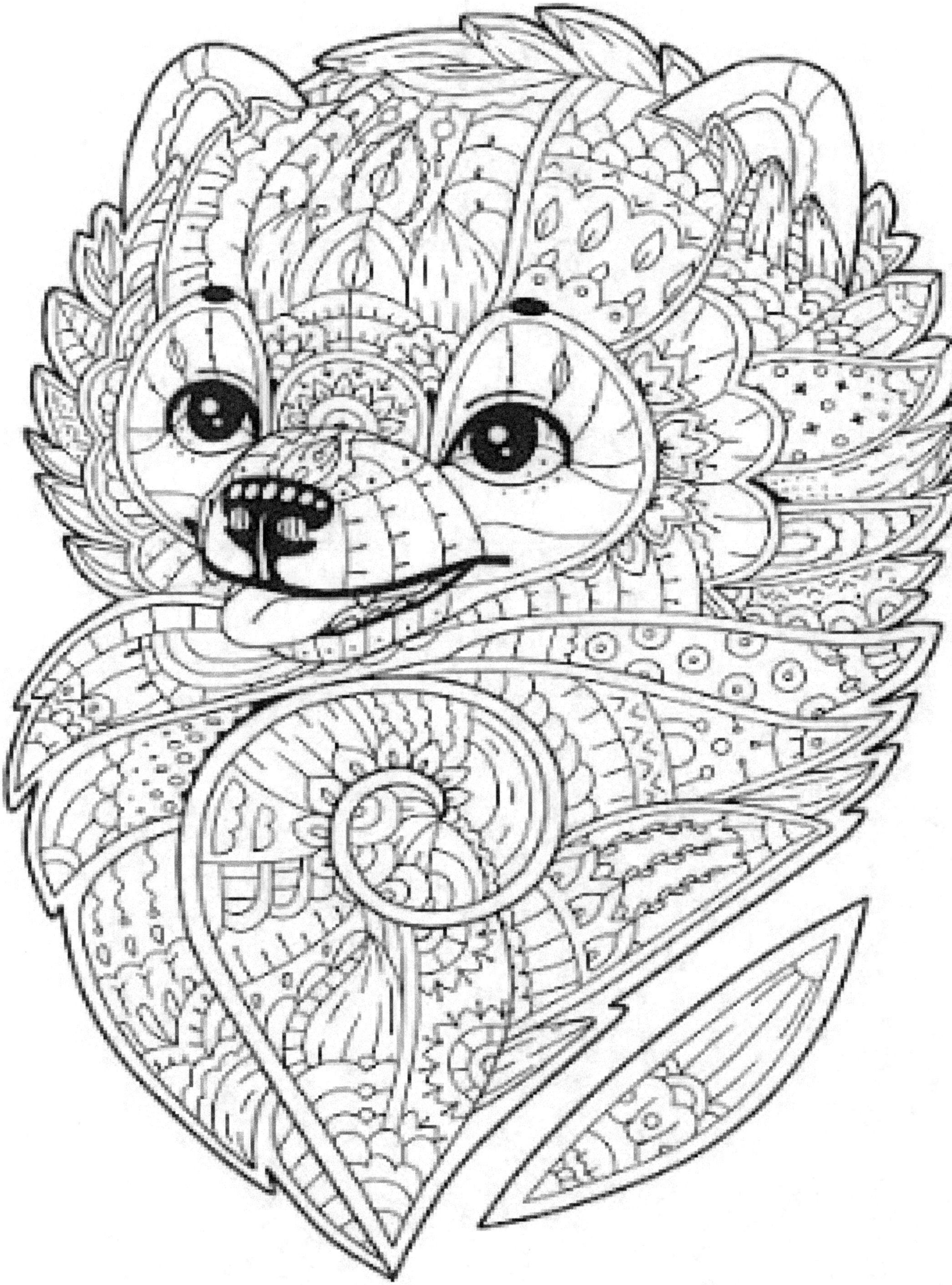

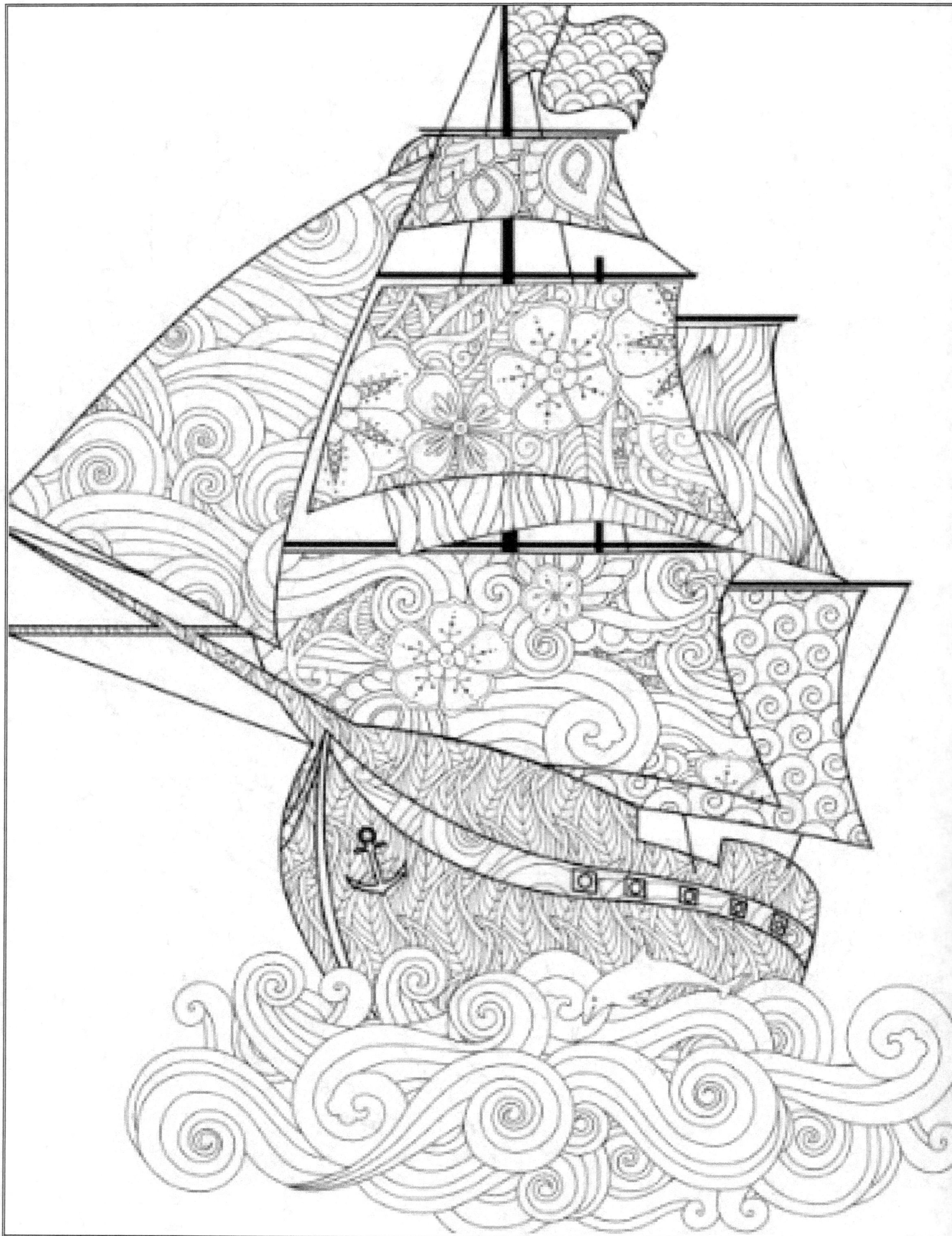

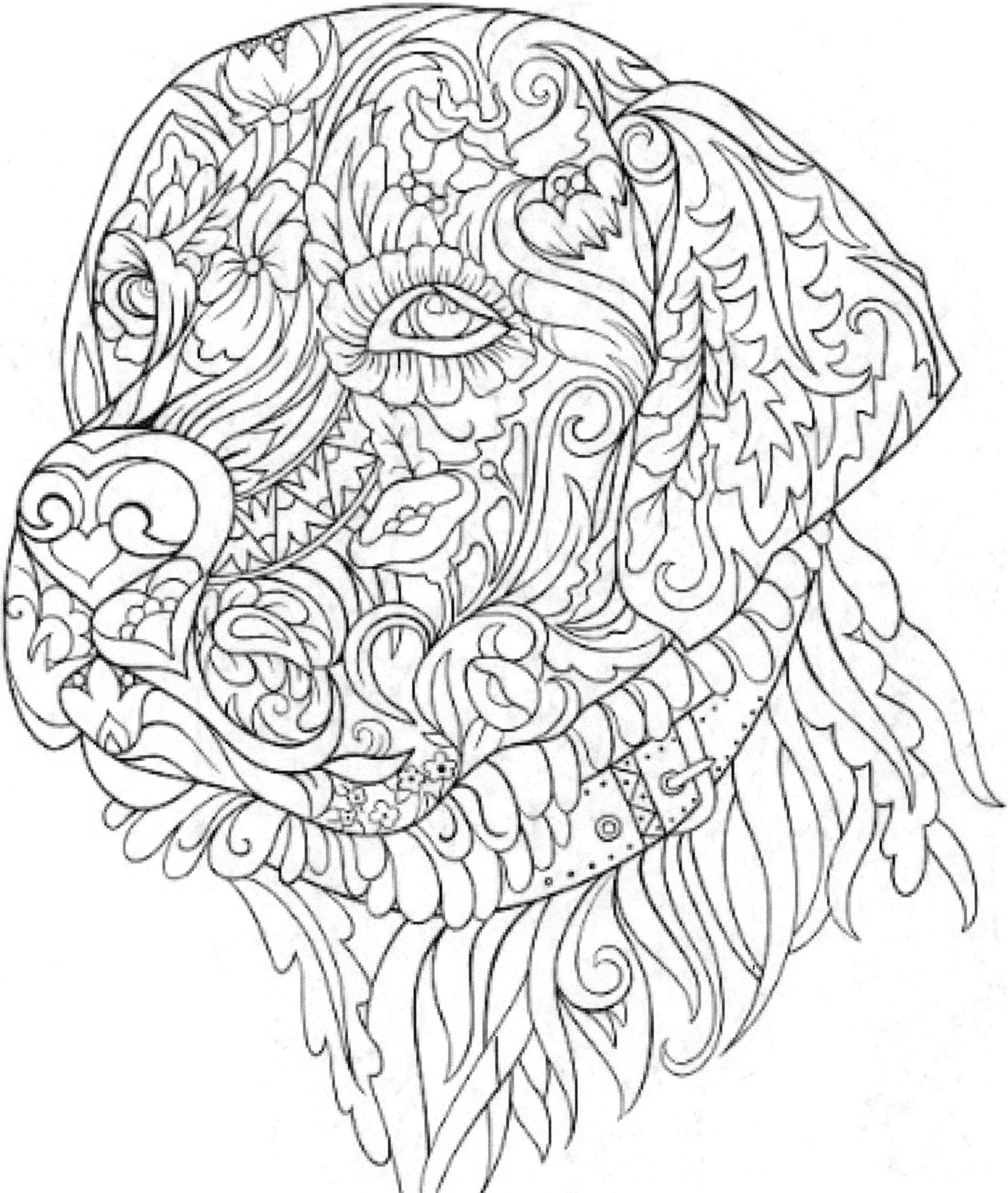

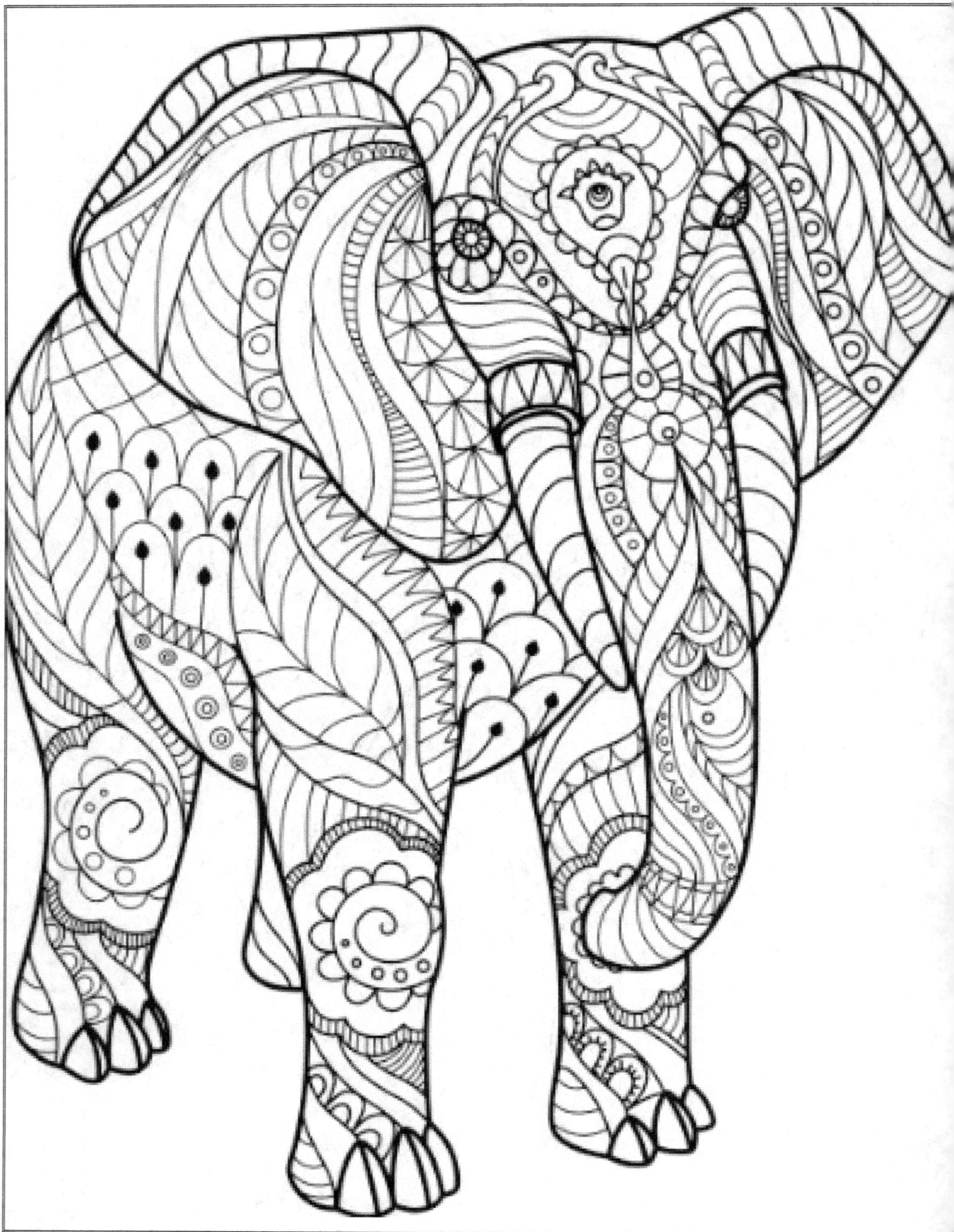

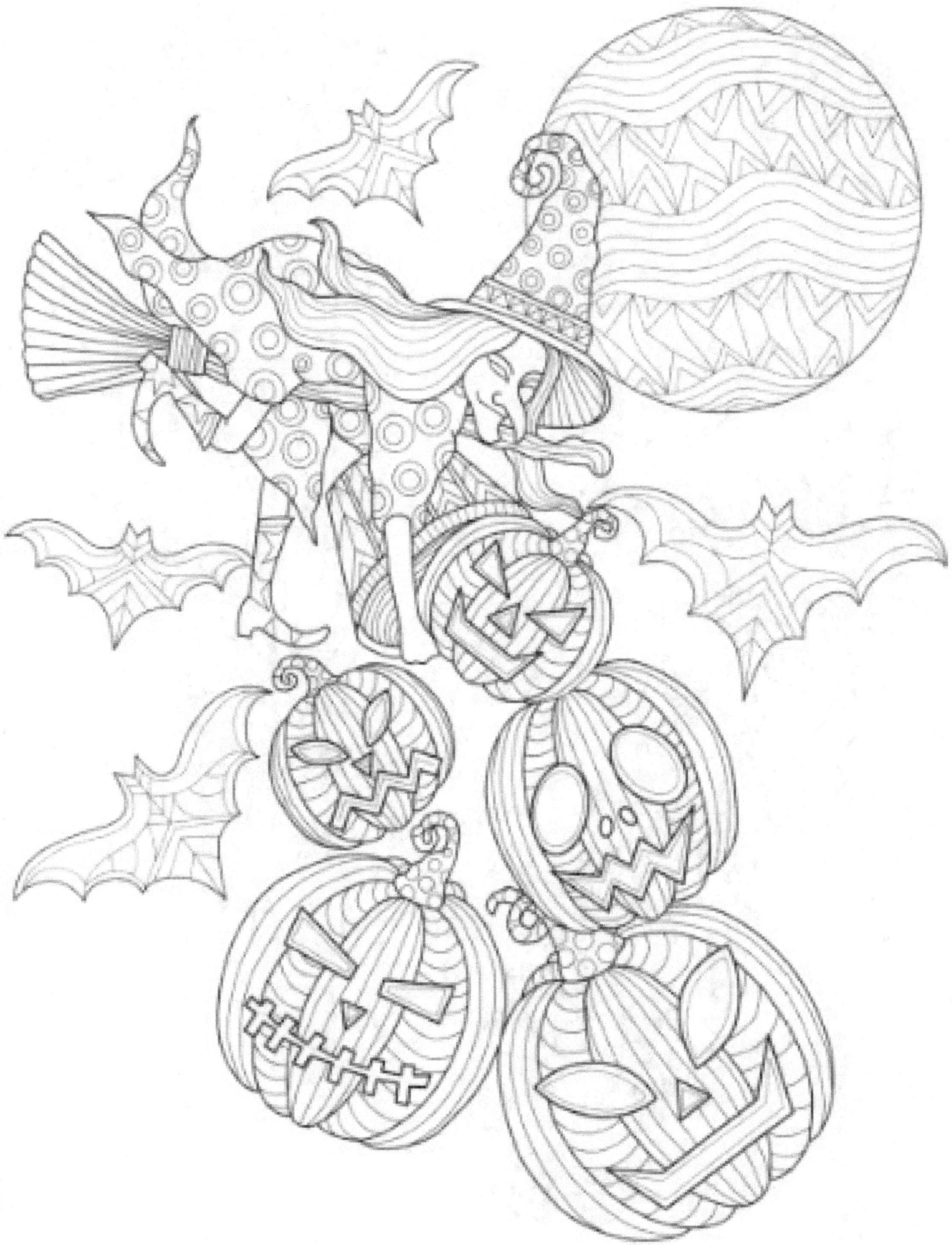

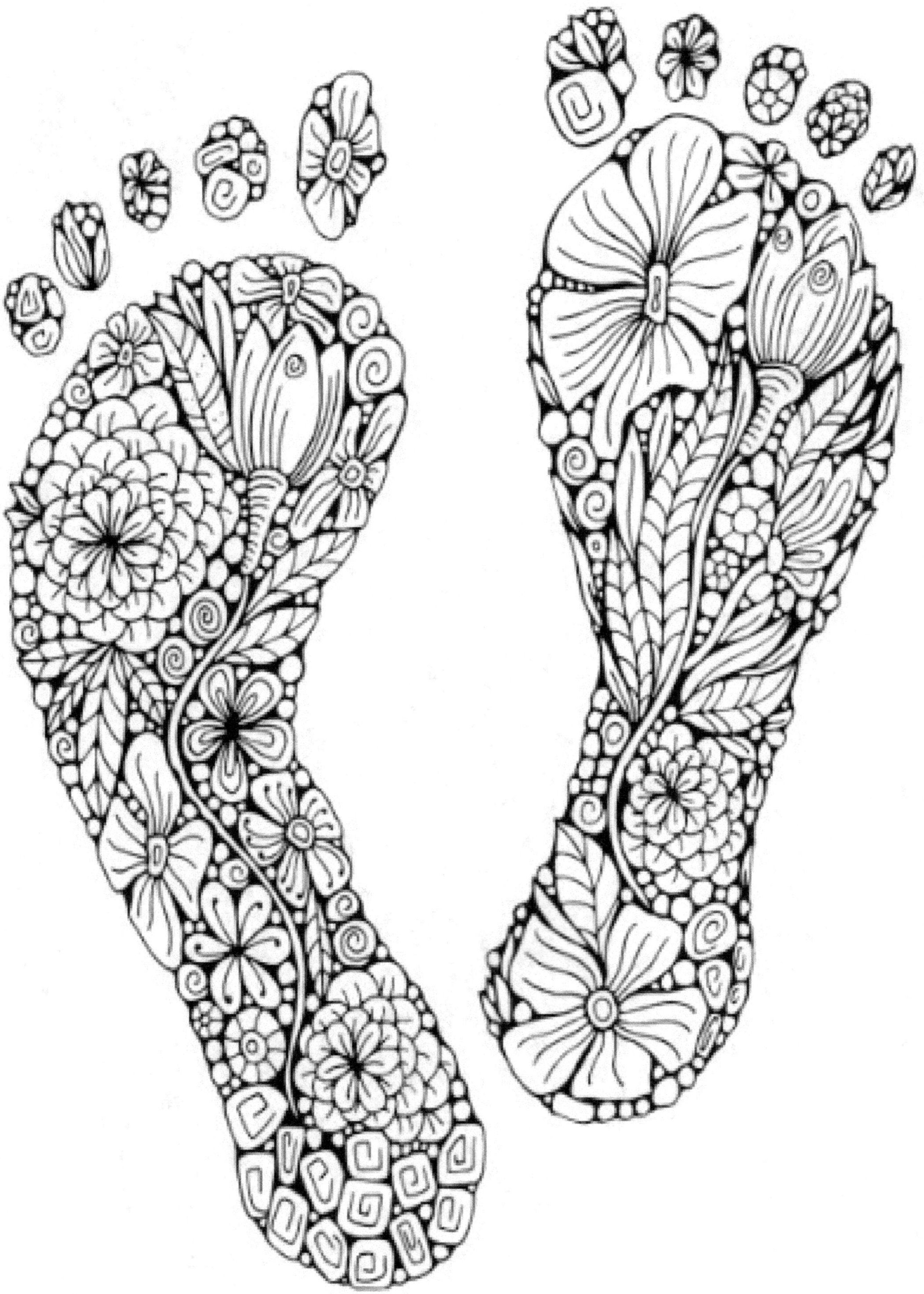

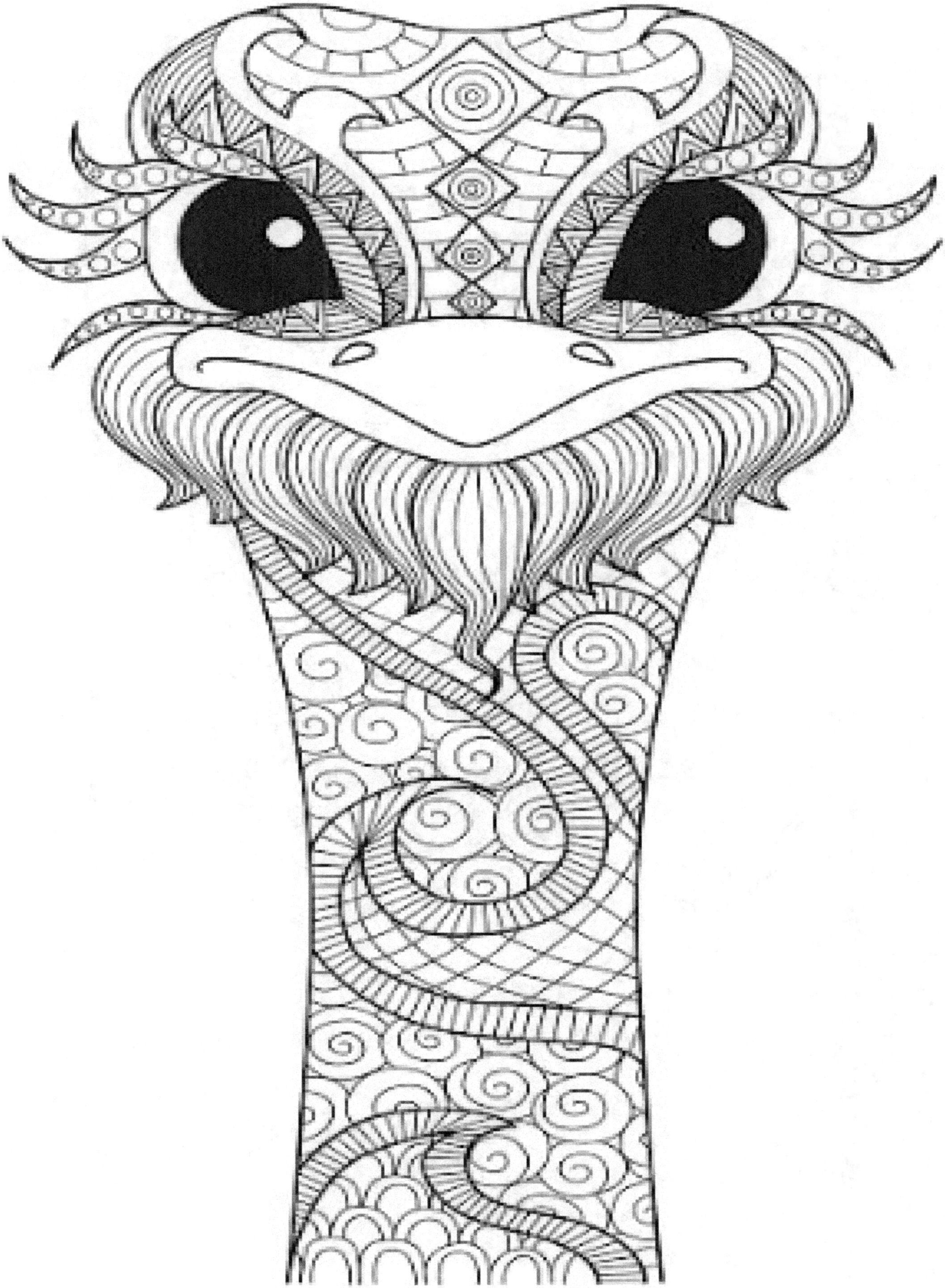

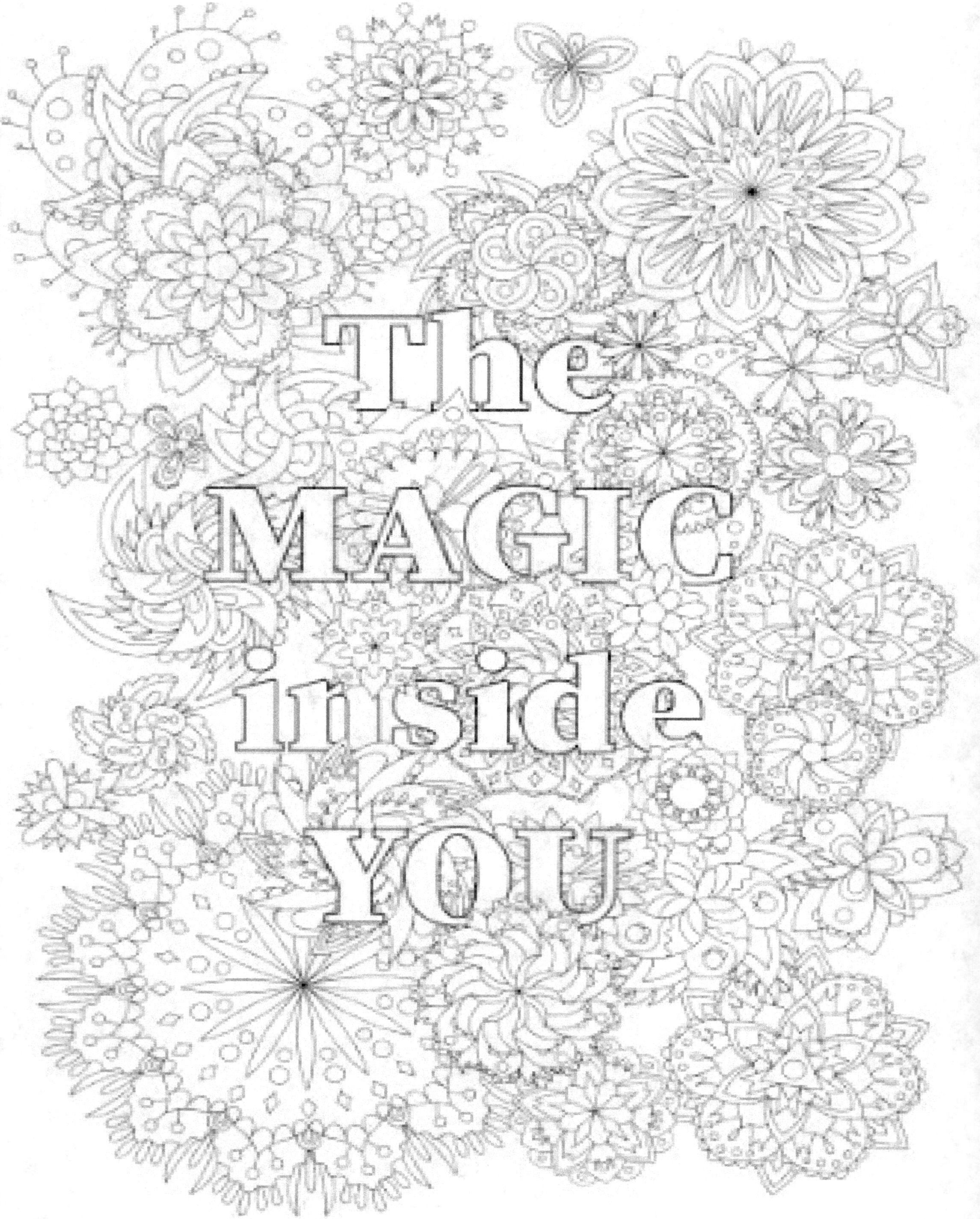
The
MAGIC
inside
YOU

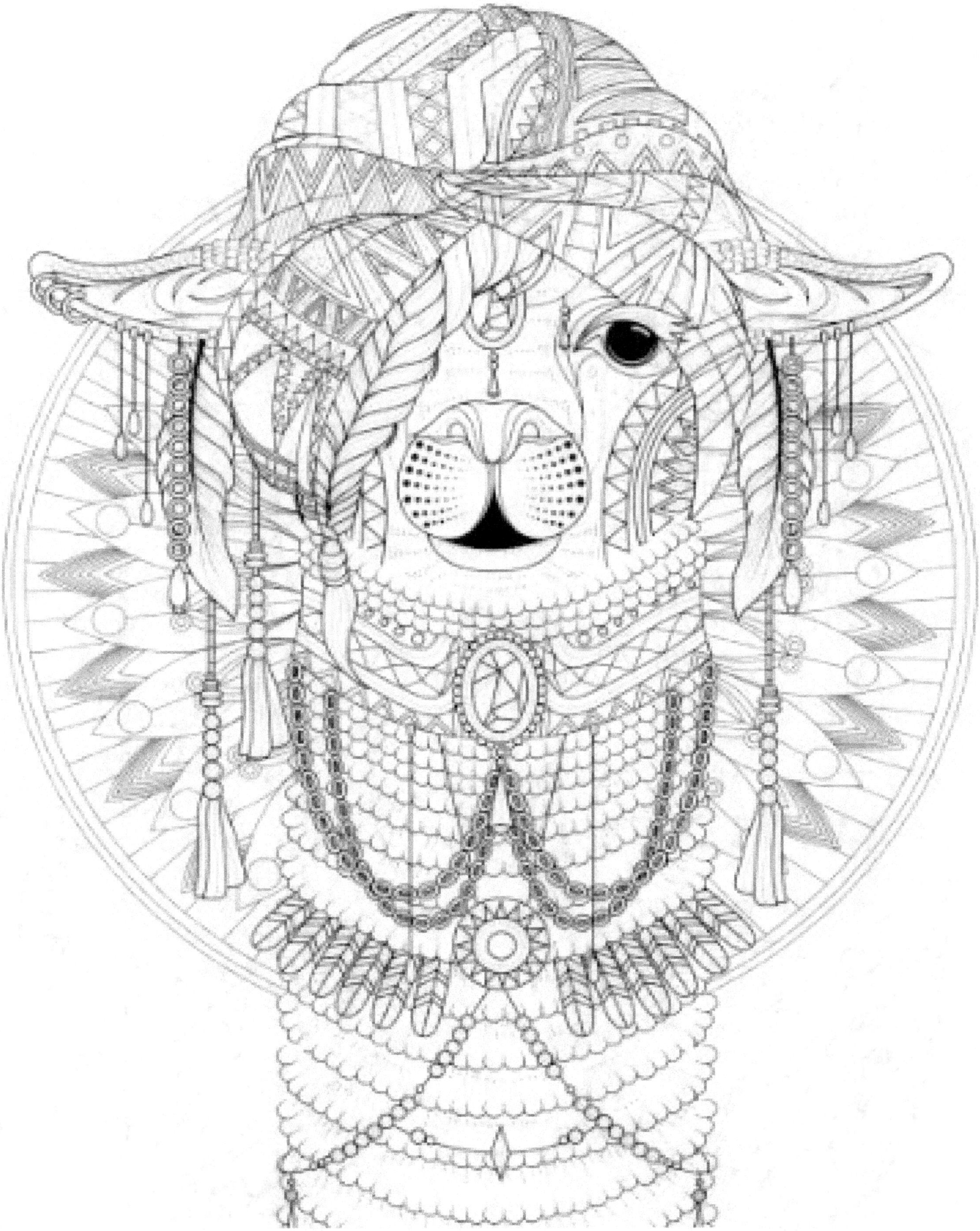

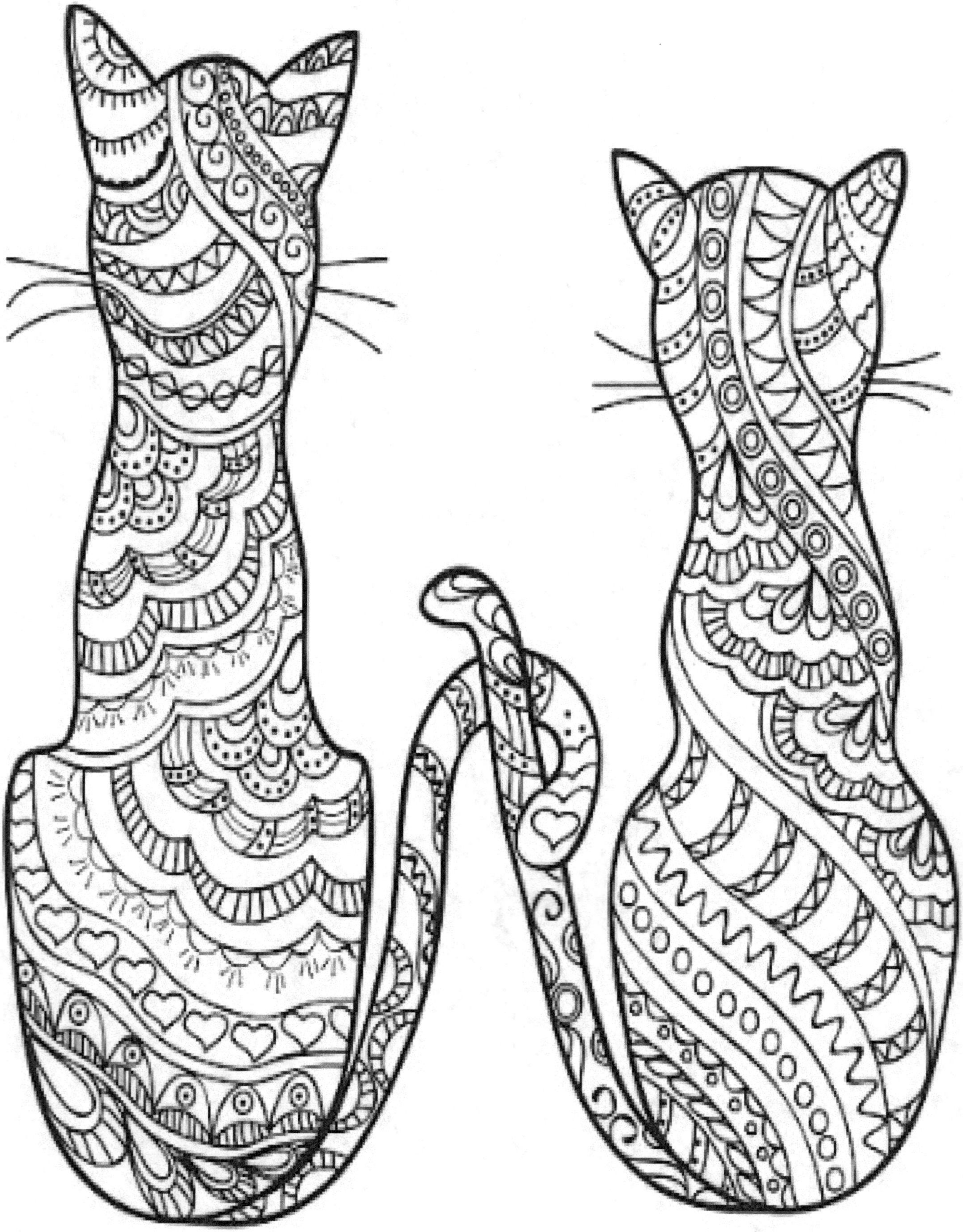

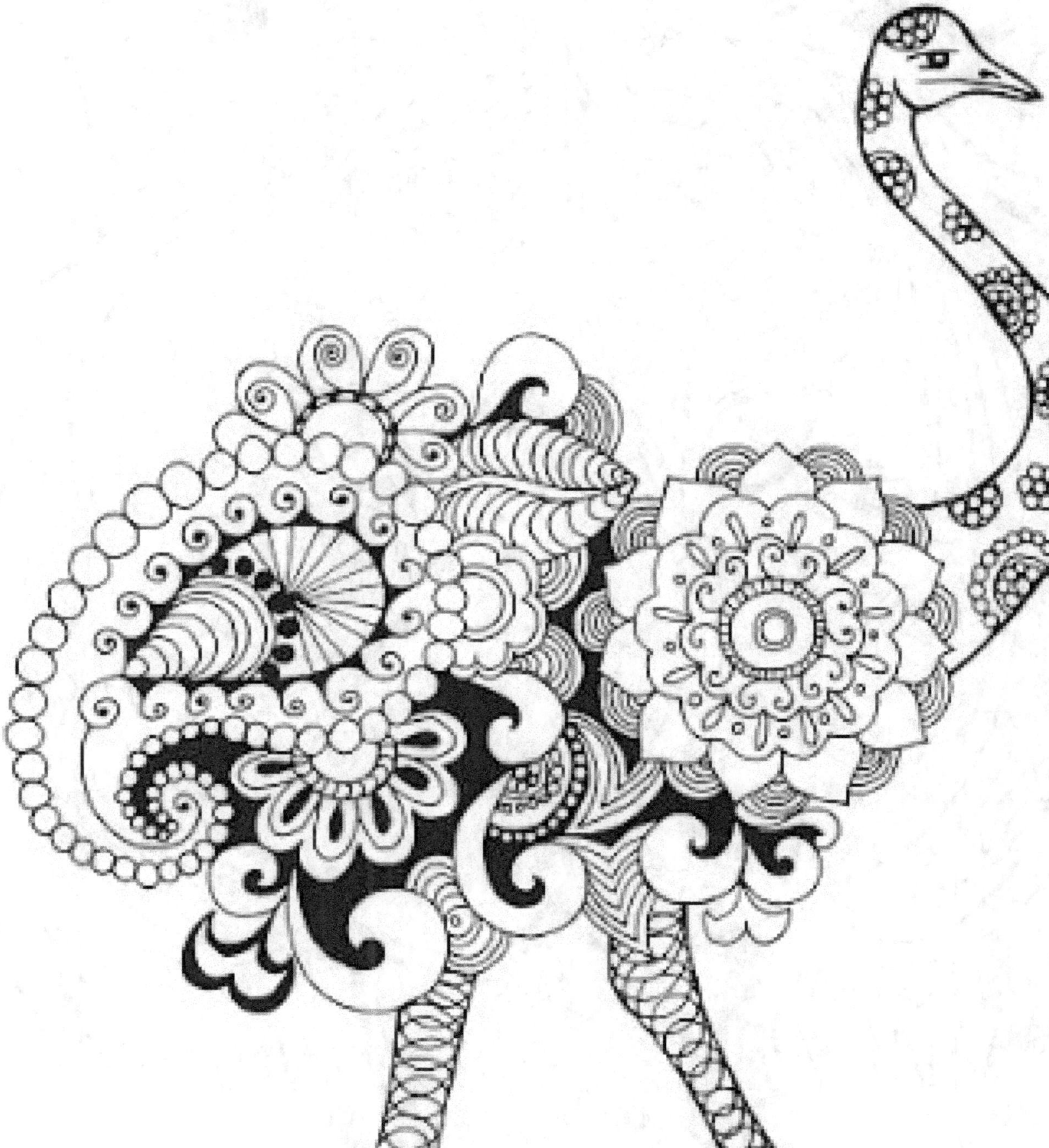

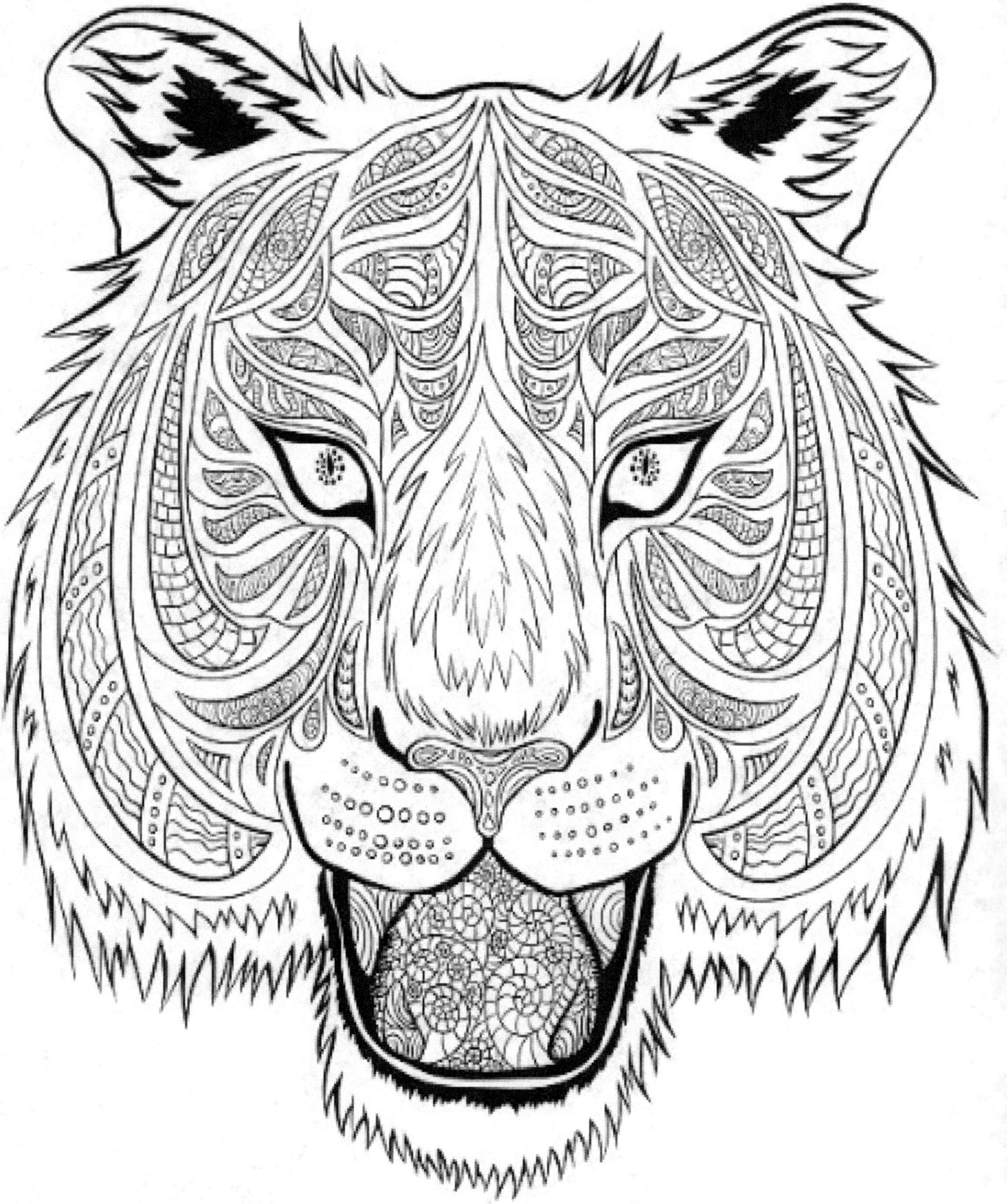

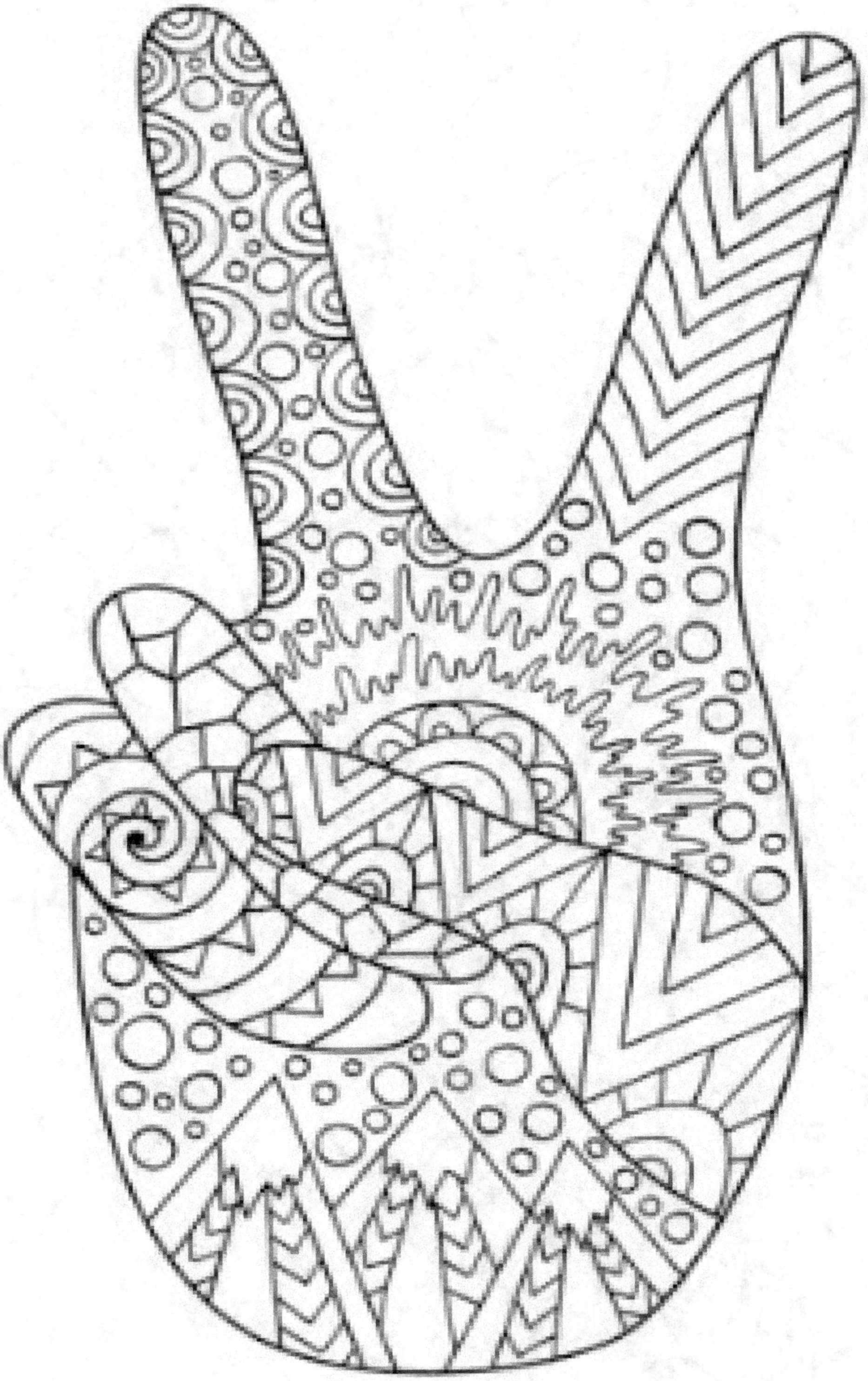

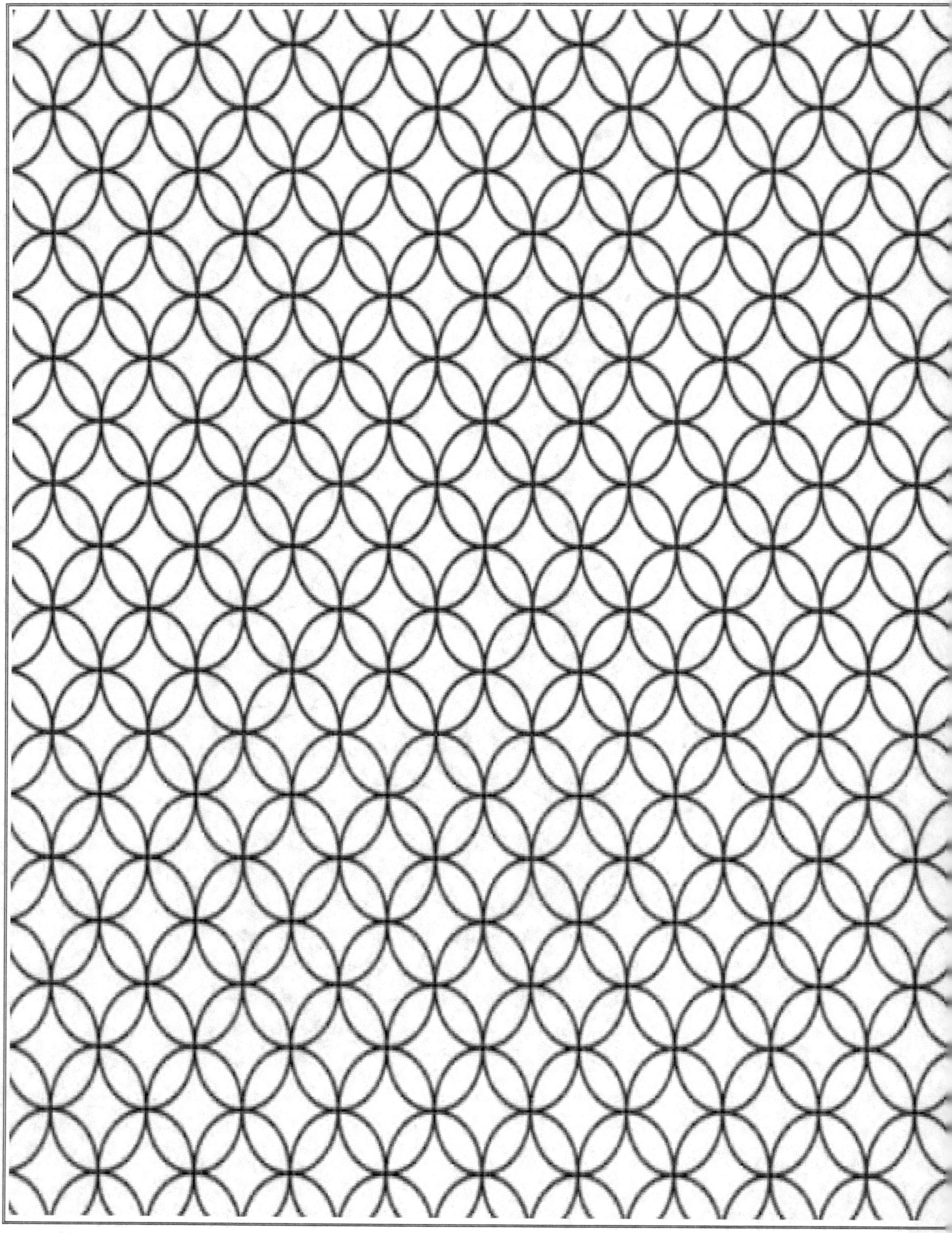

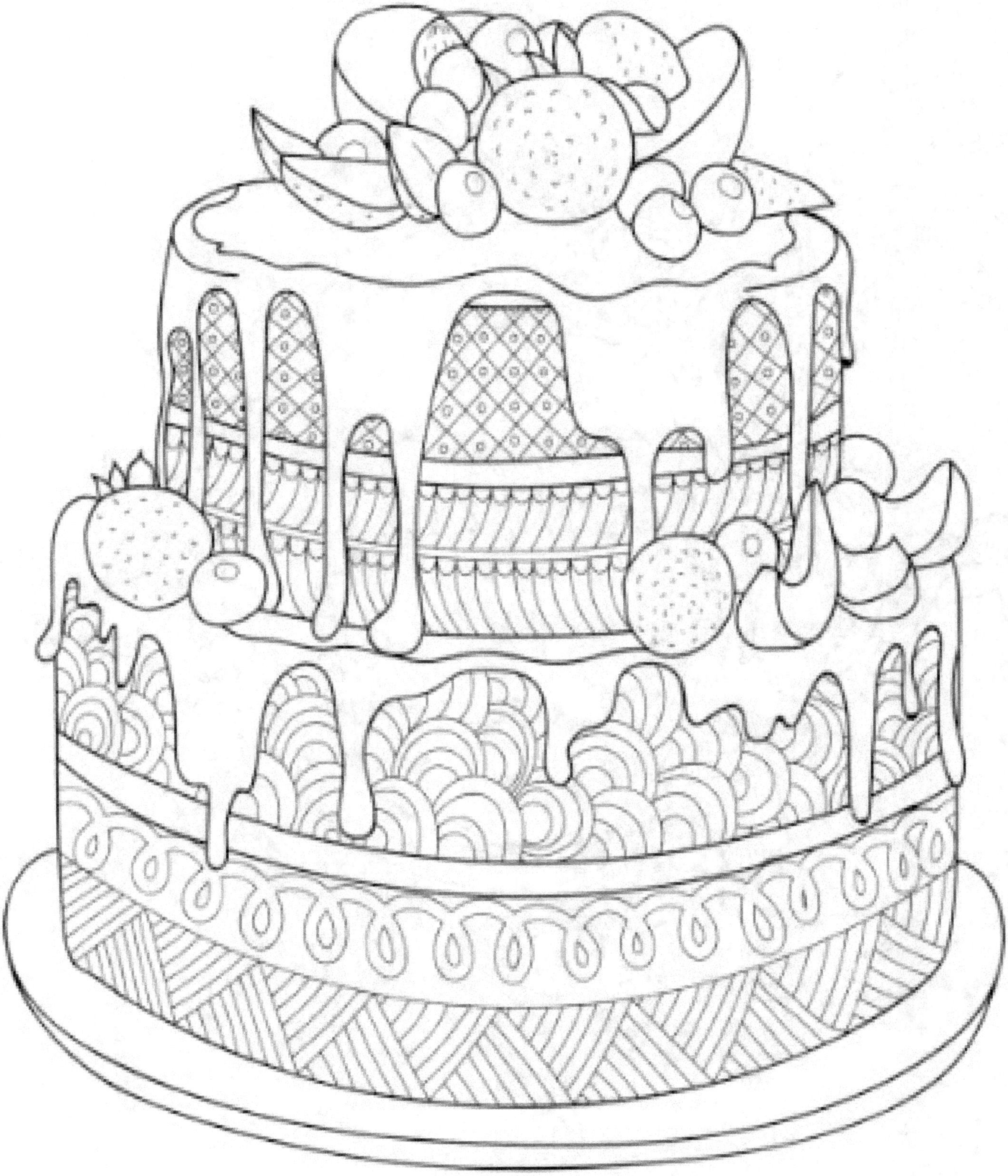

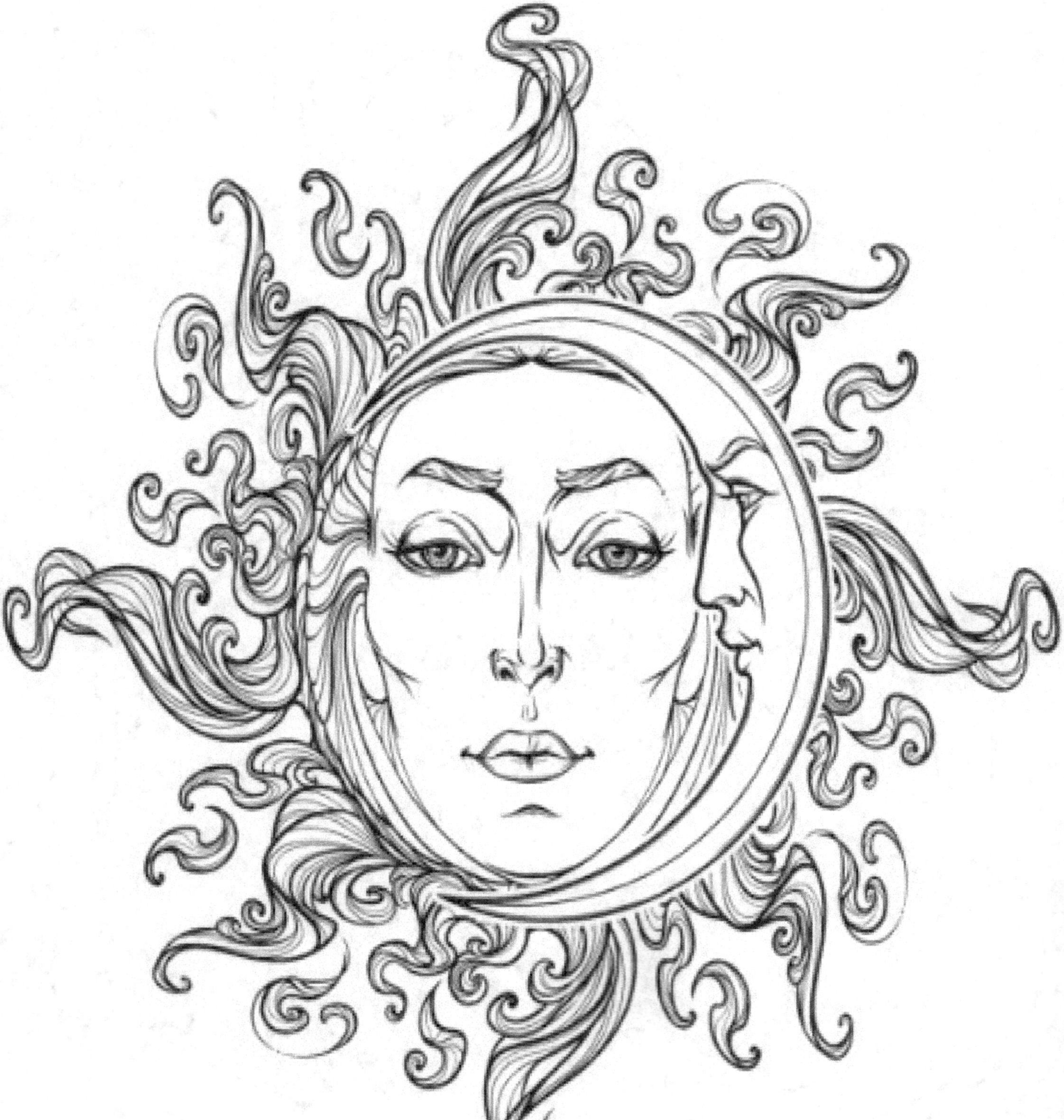

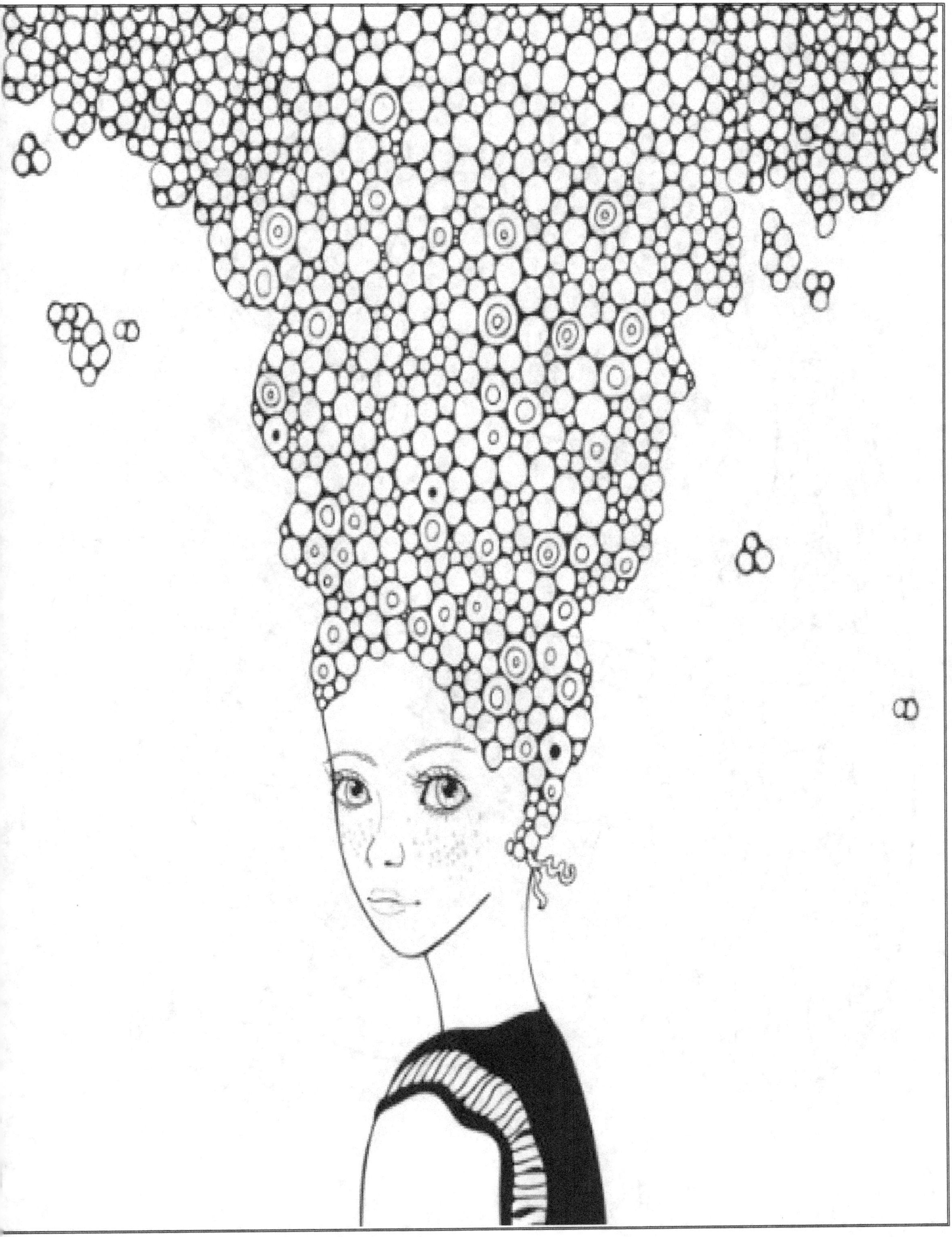

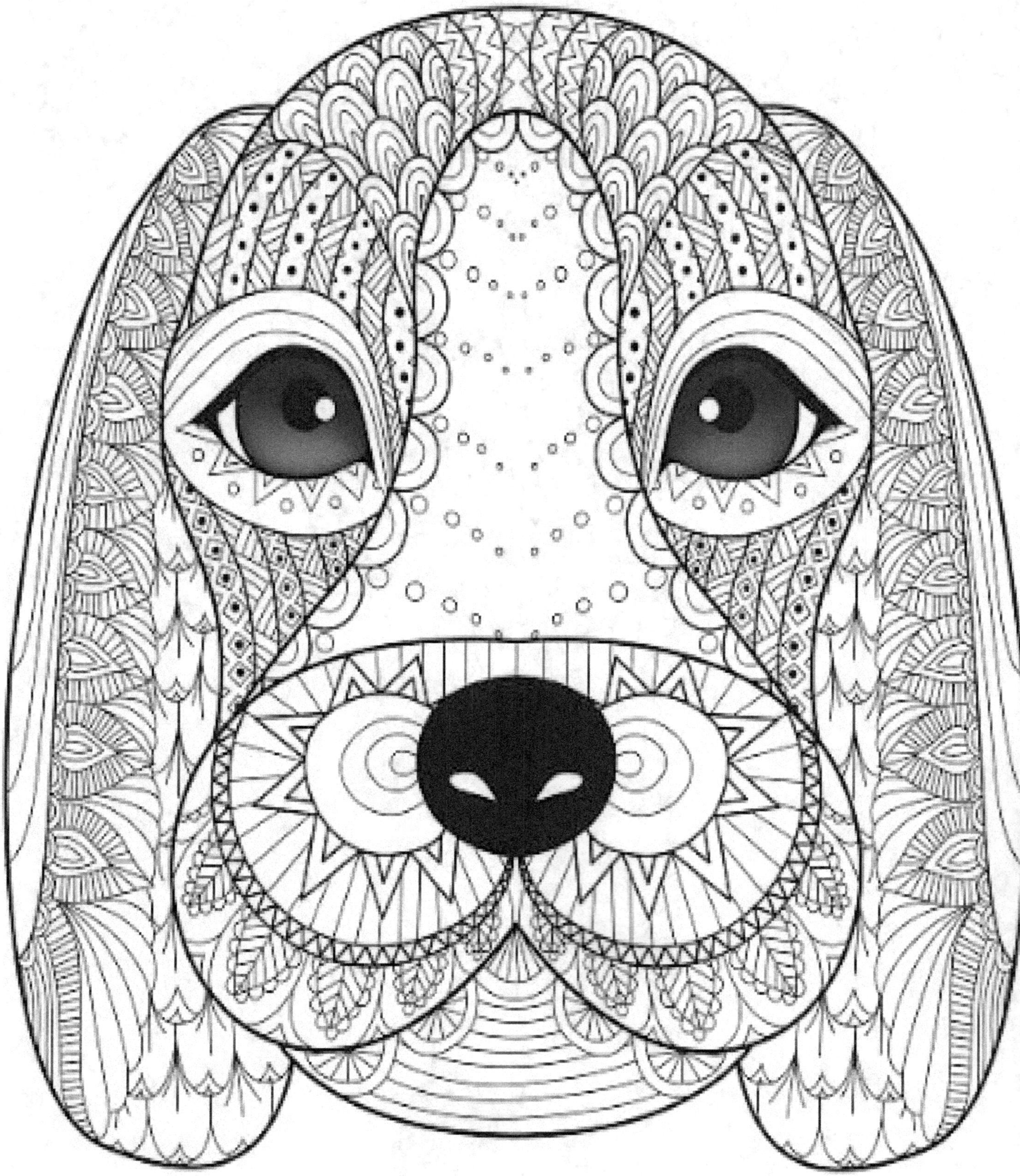

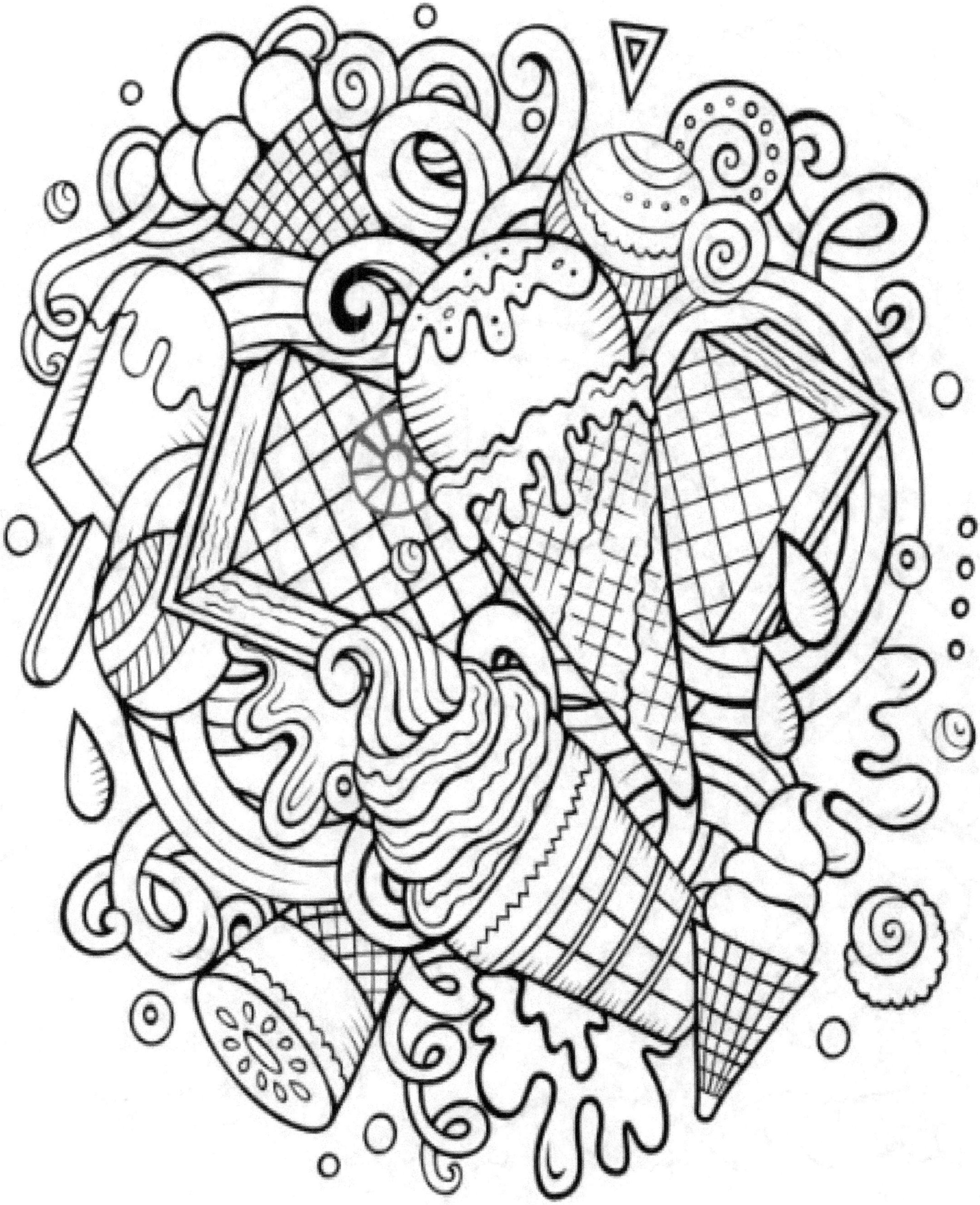

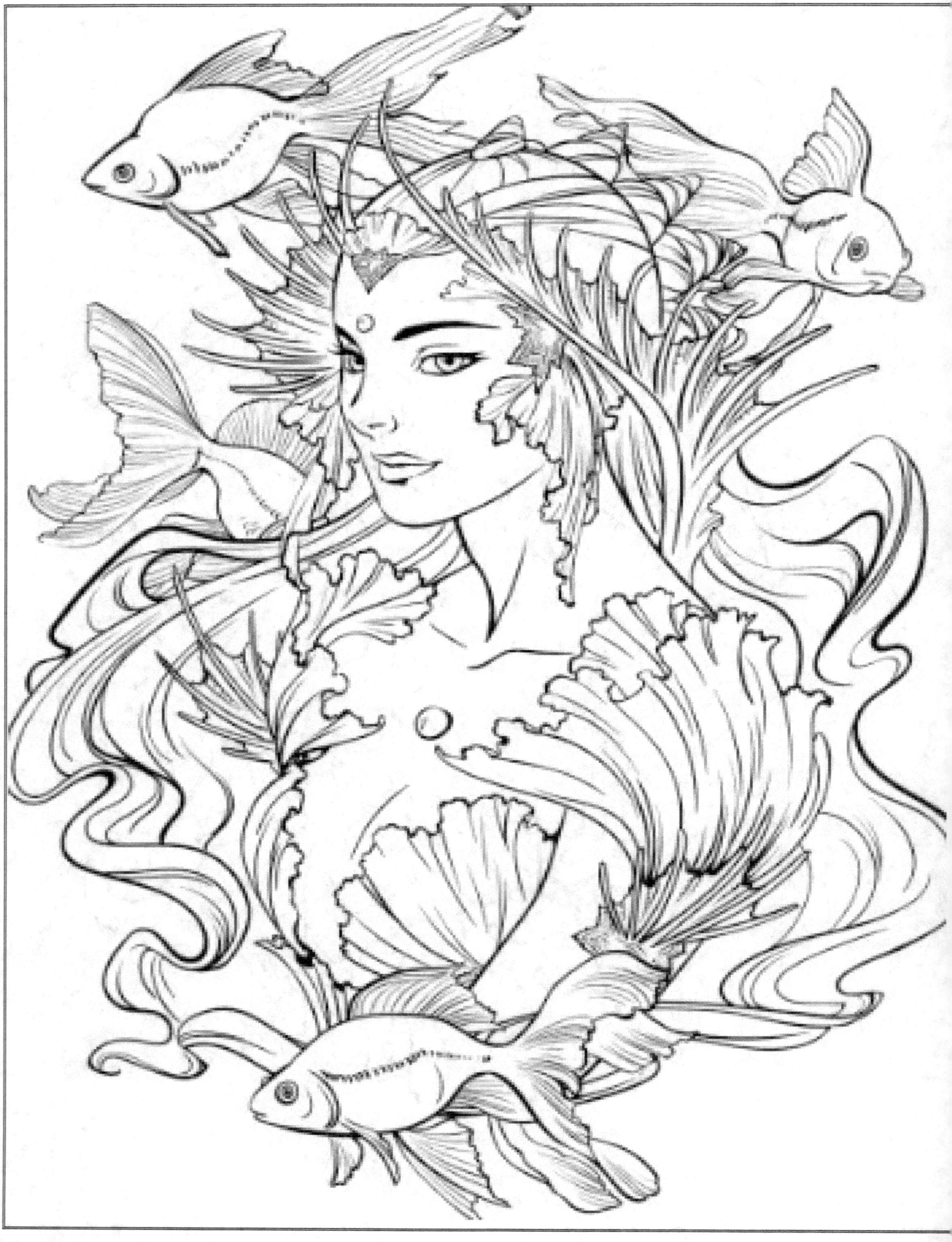

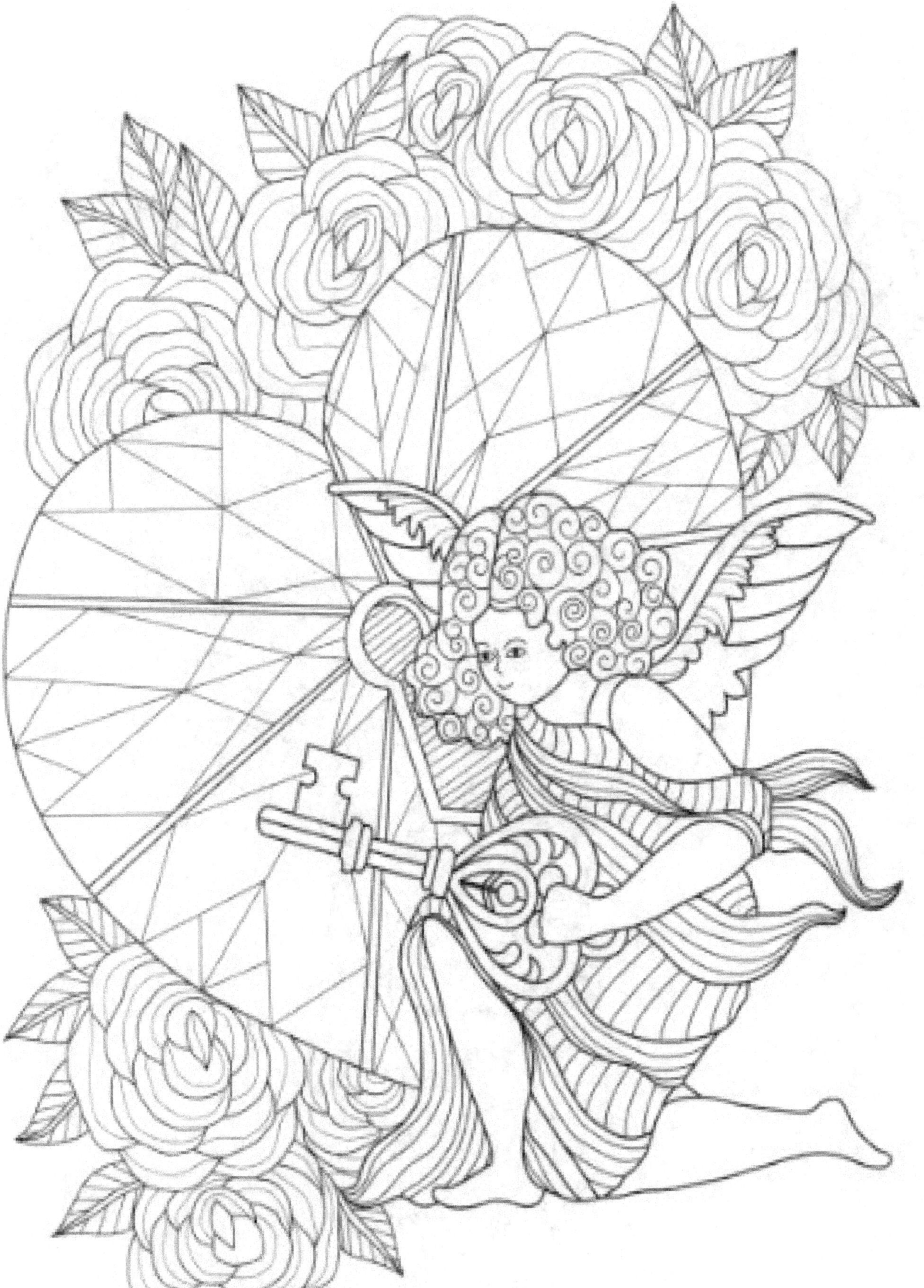

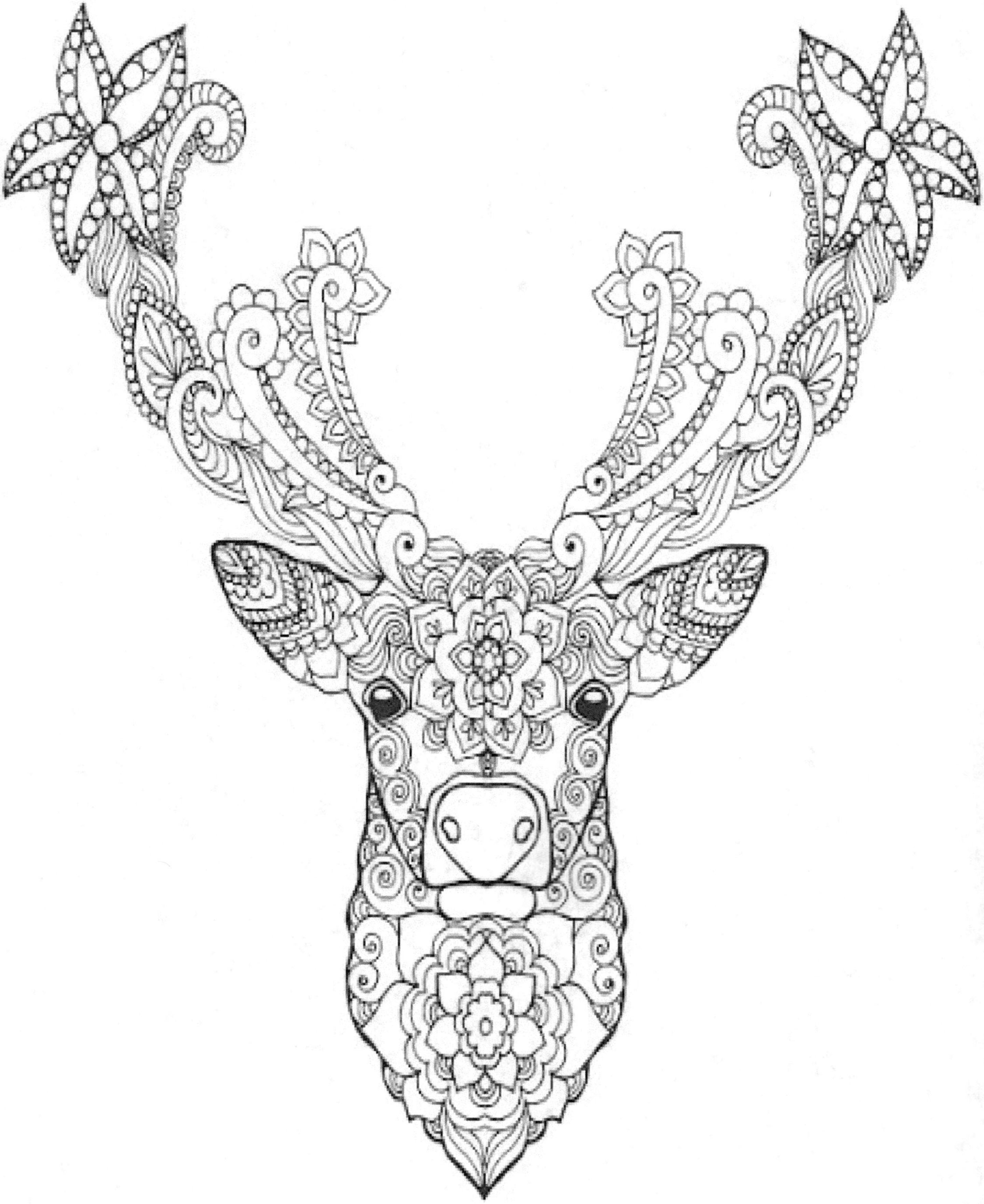

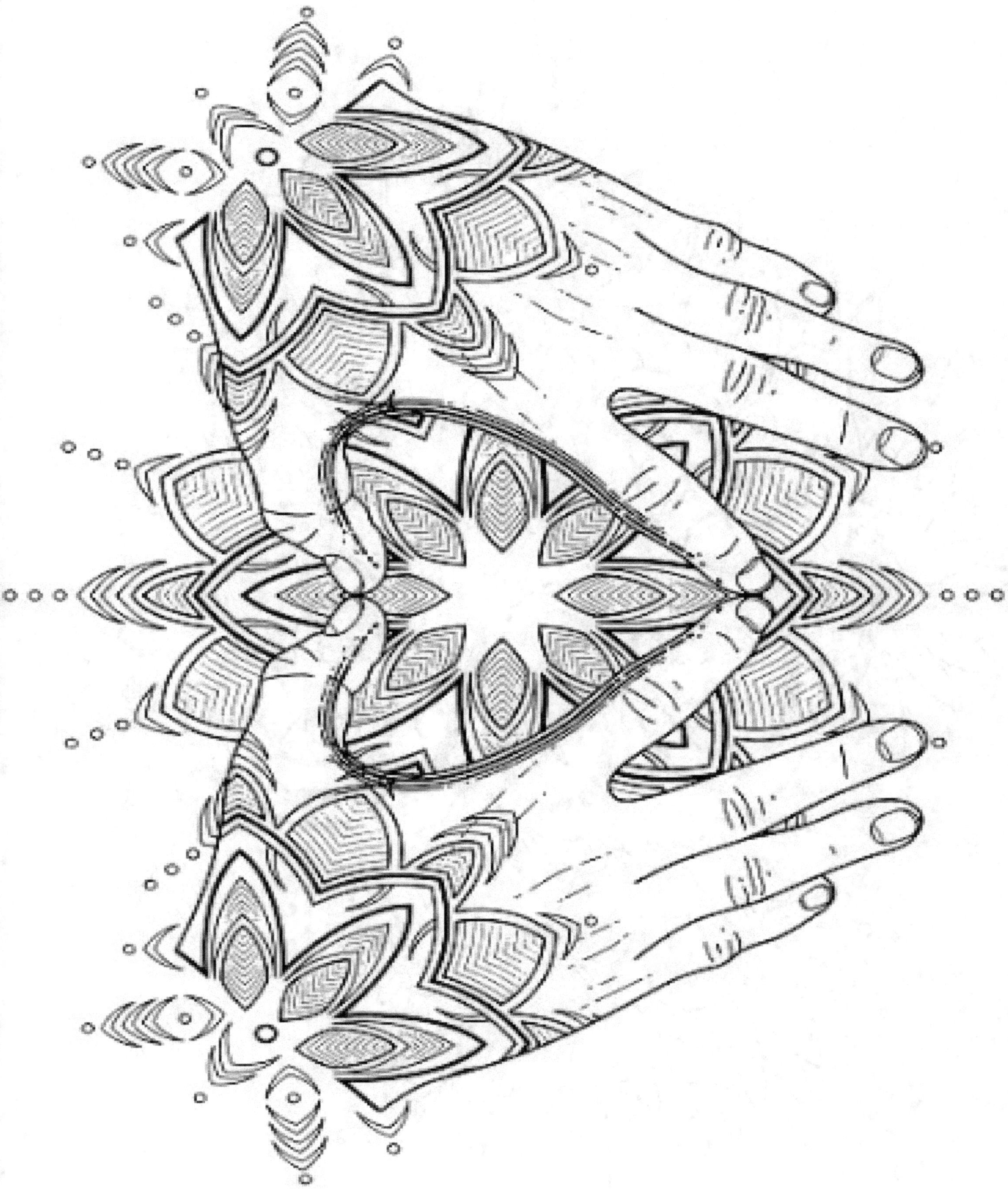

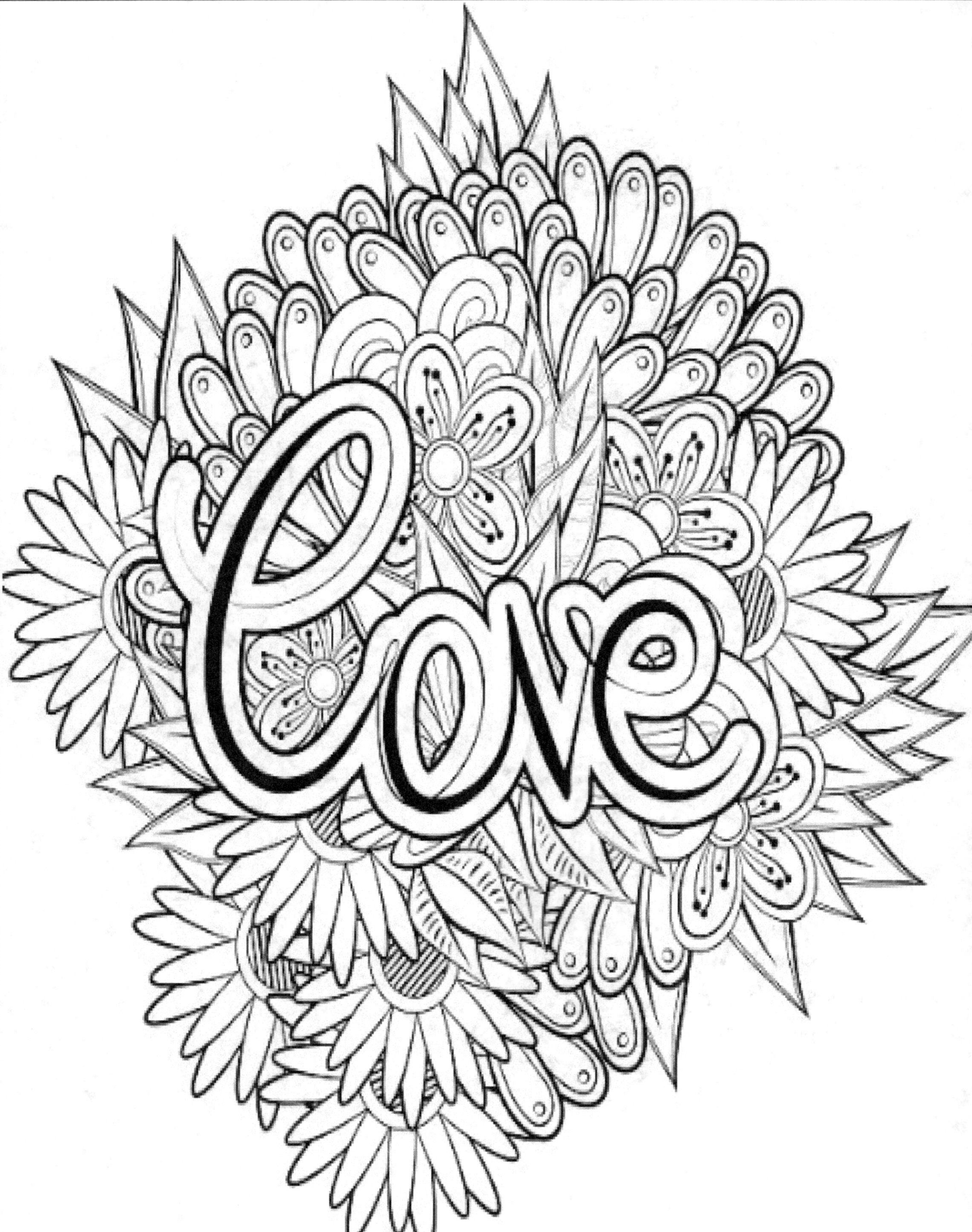
Love

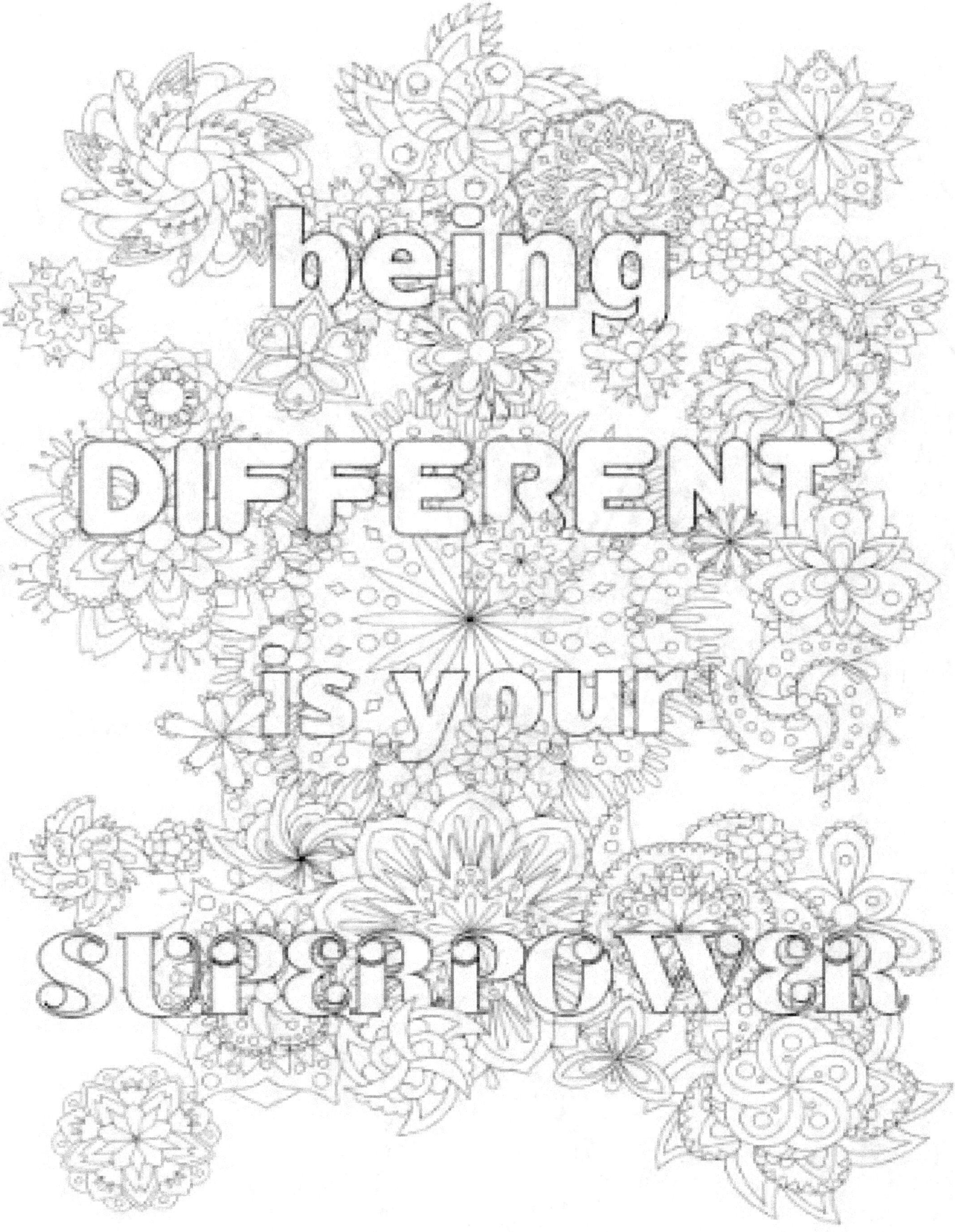
being
DIFFERENT
is your
SUPERPOWER

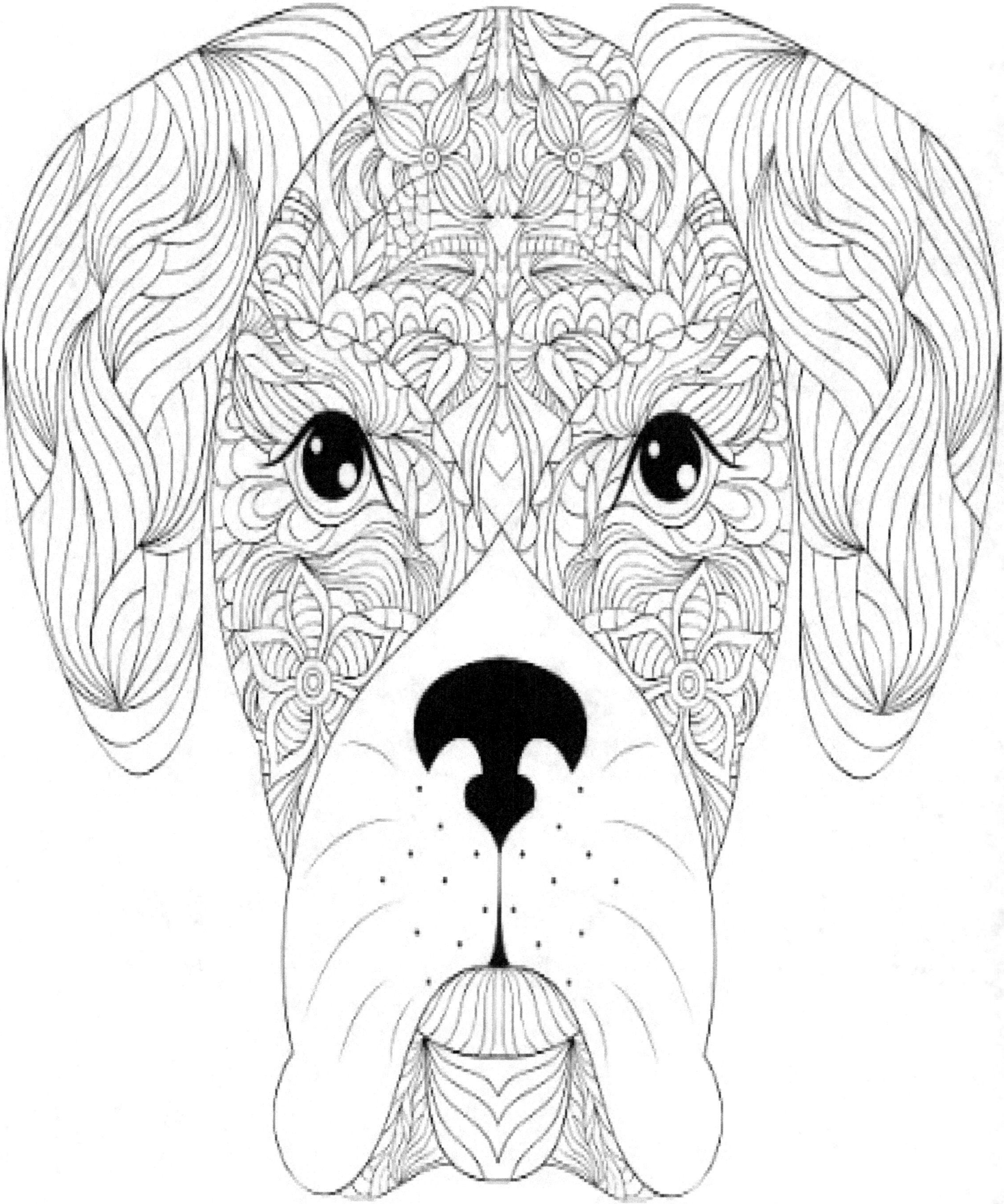

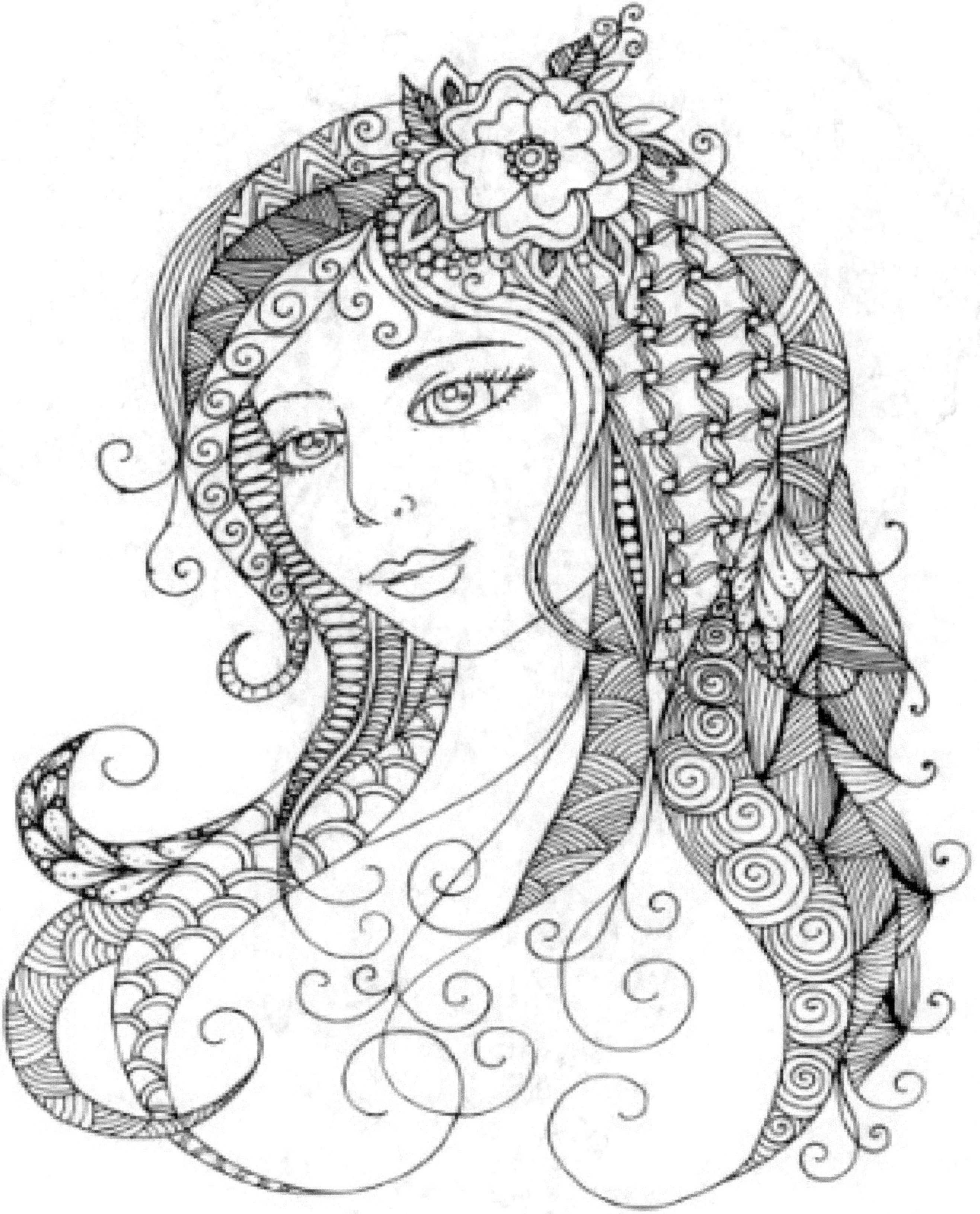

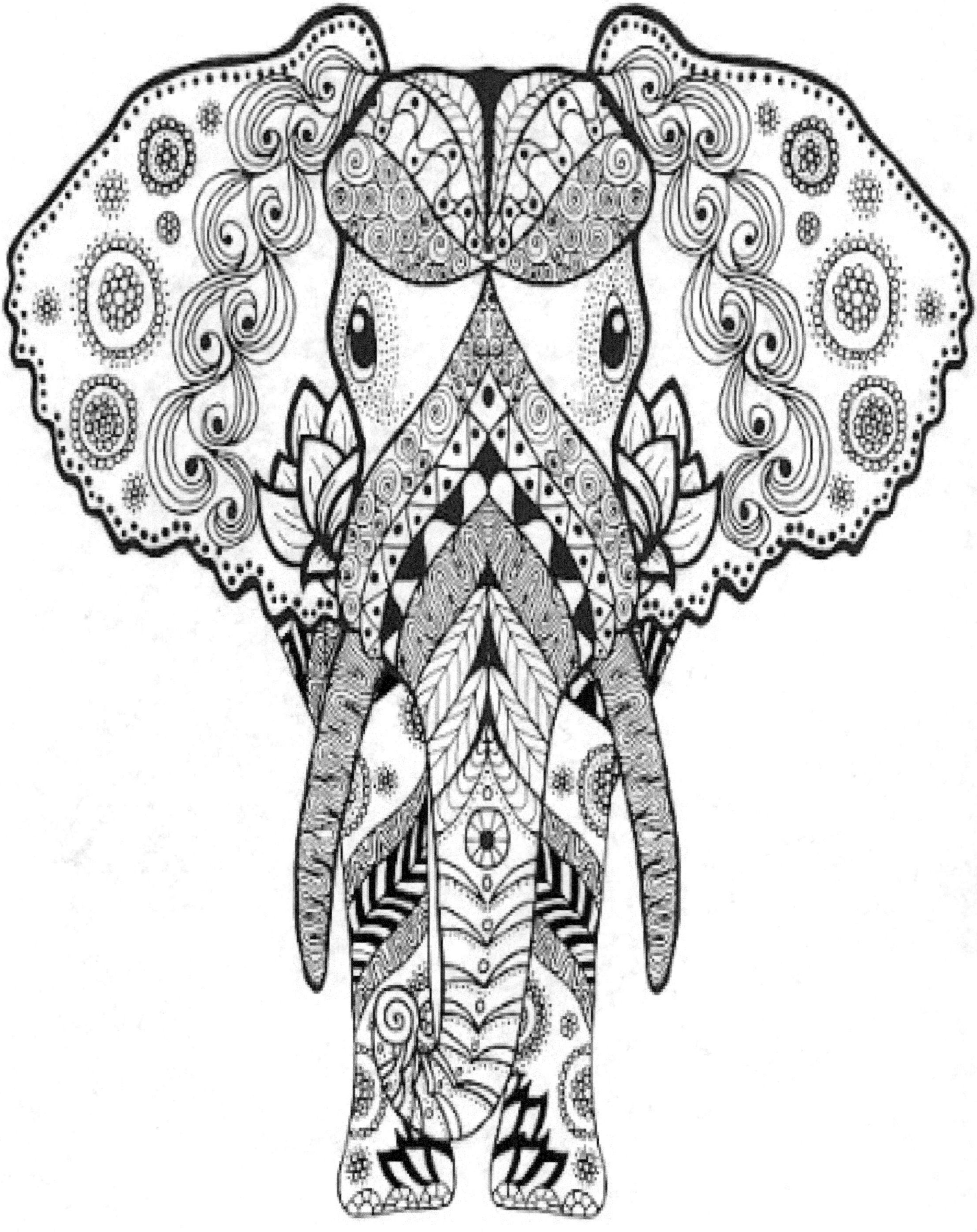

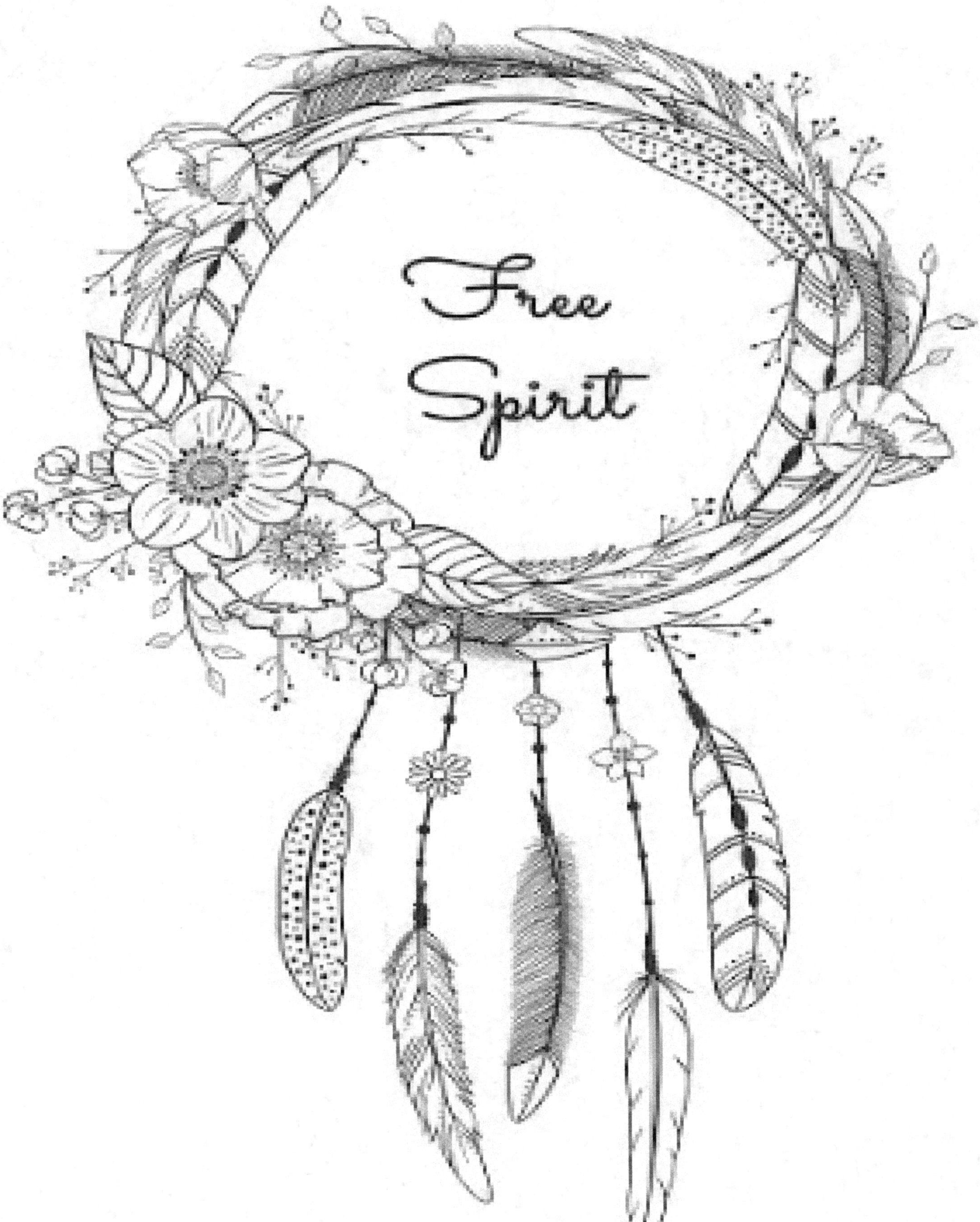
Free
Spirit

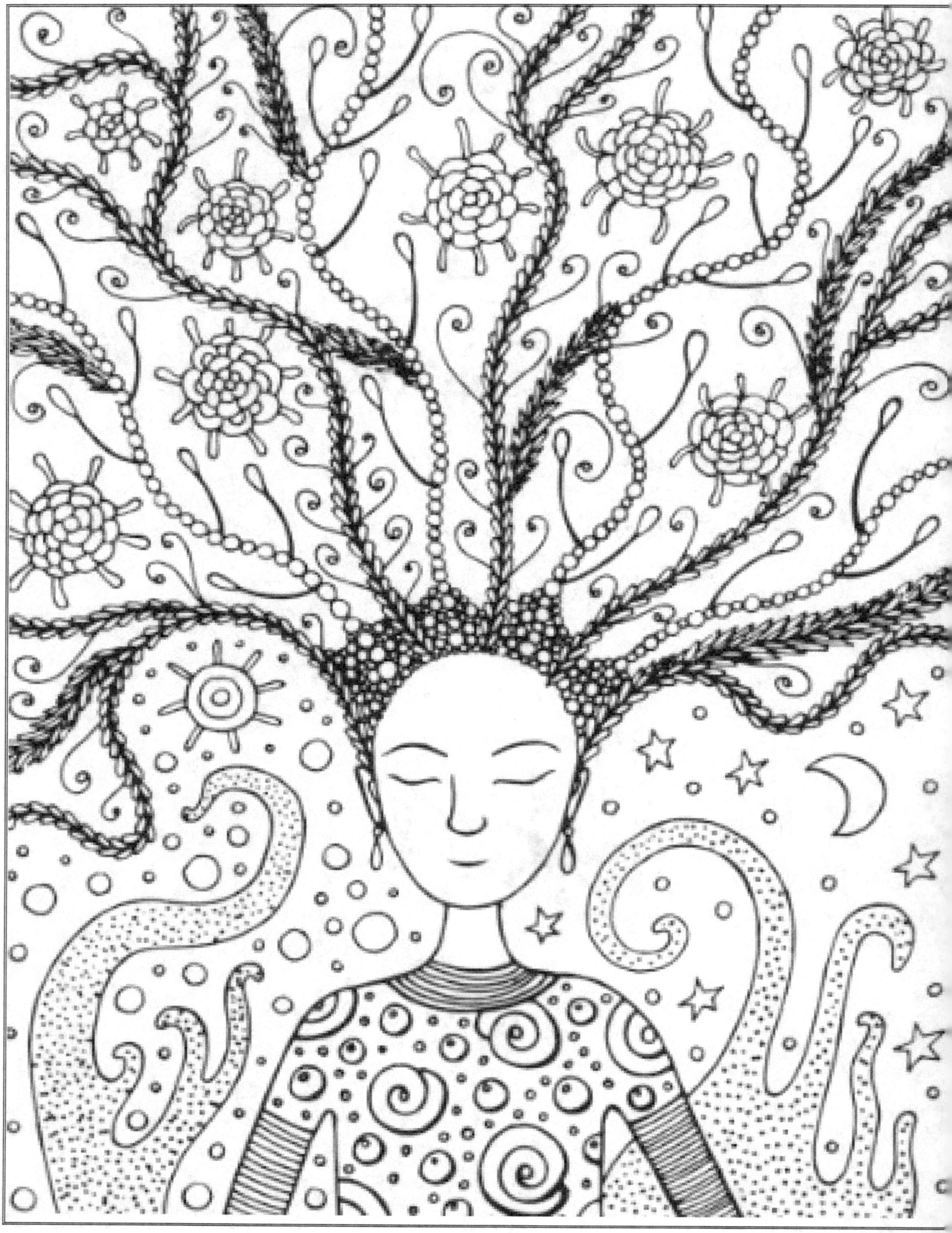

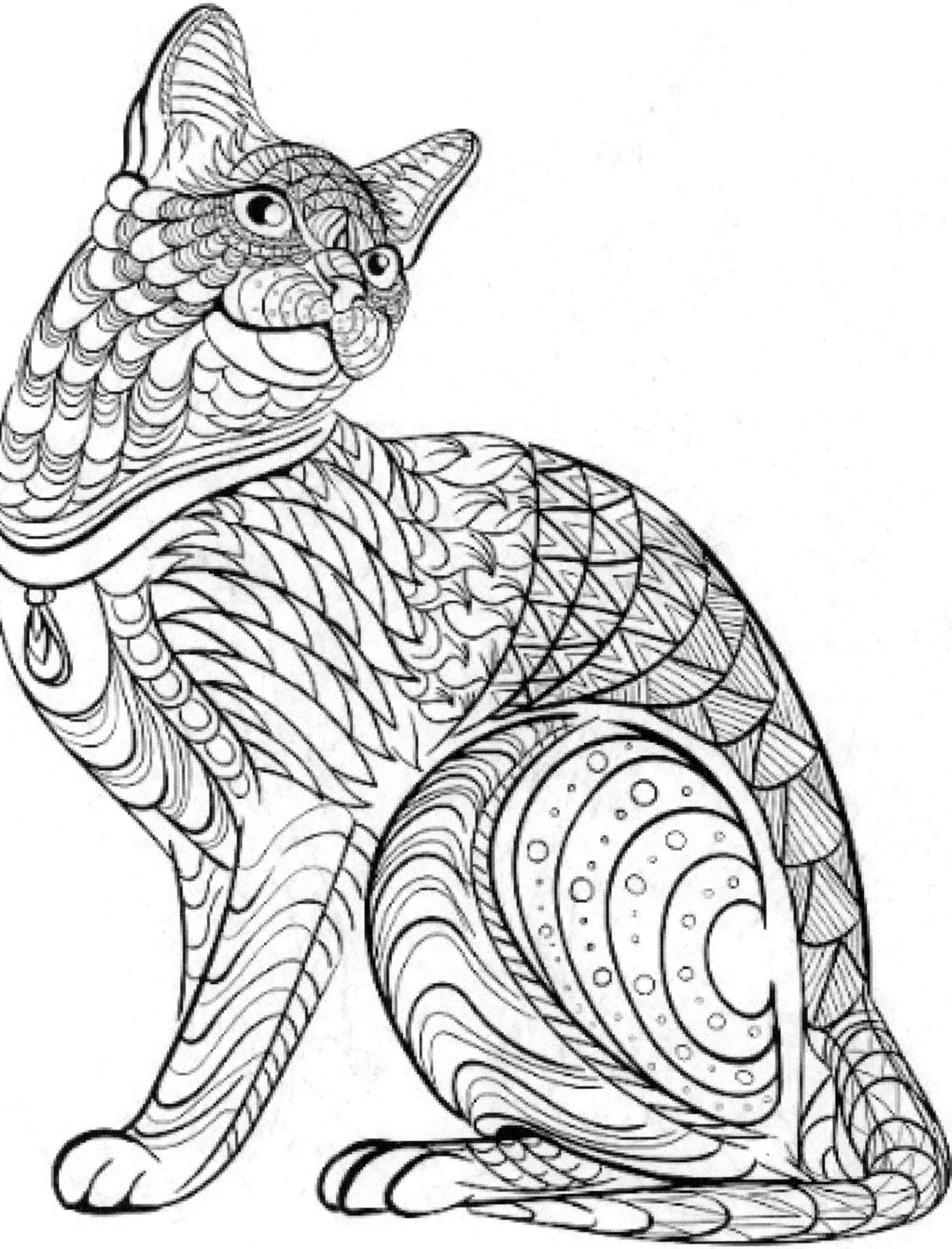

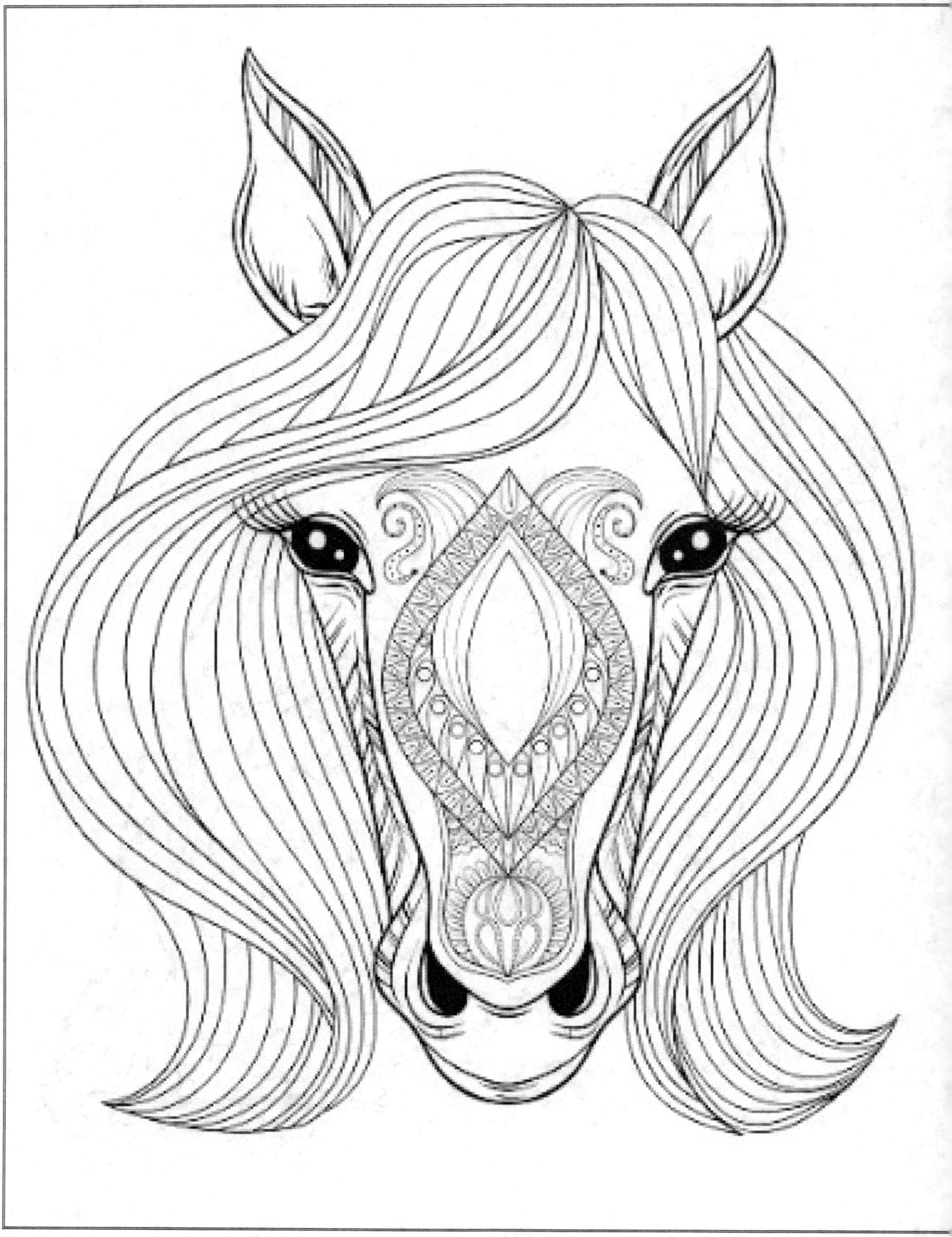

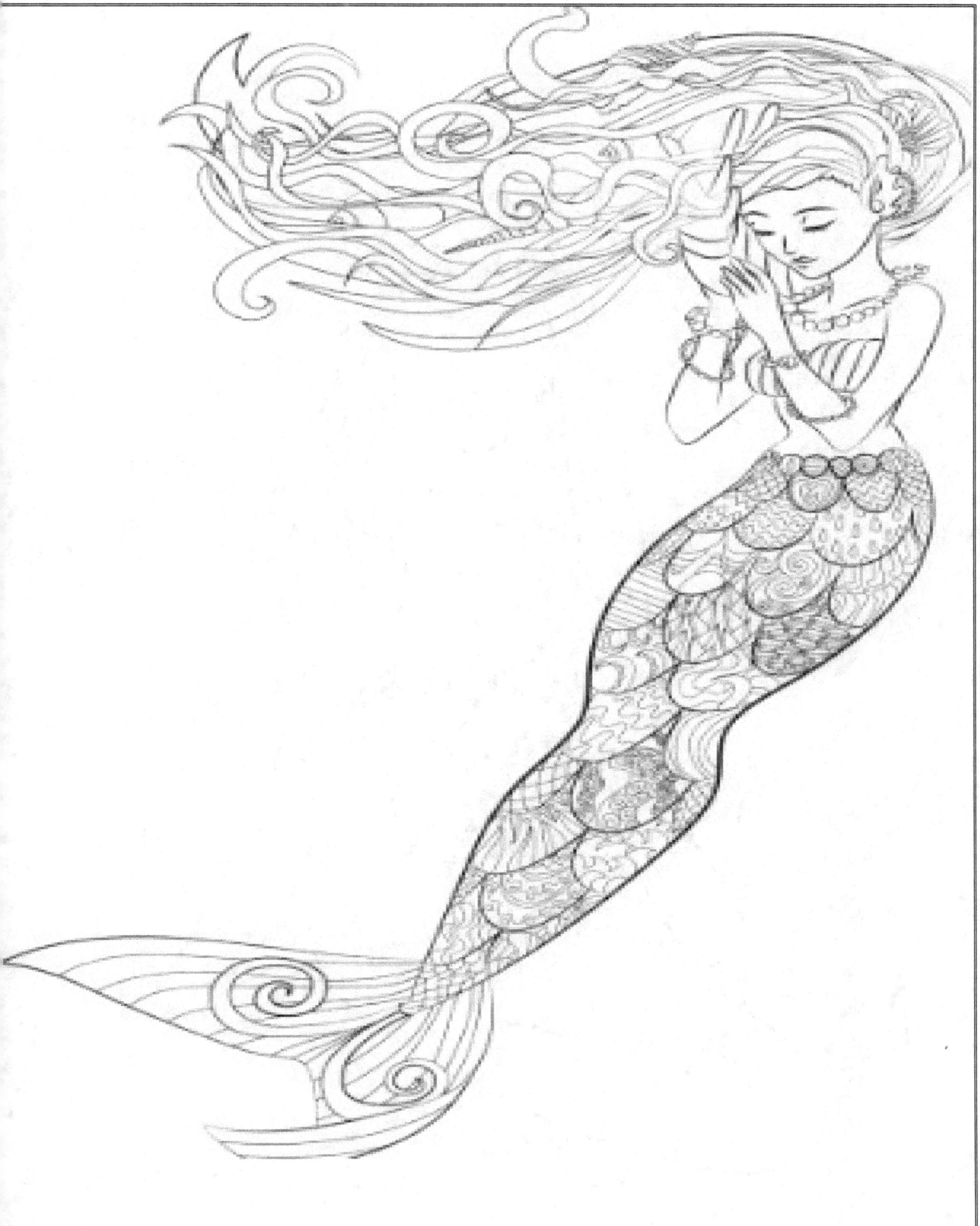

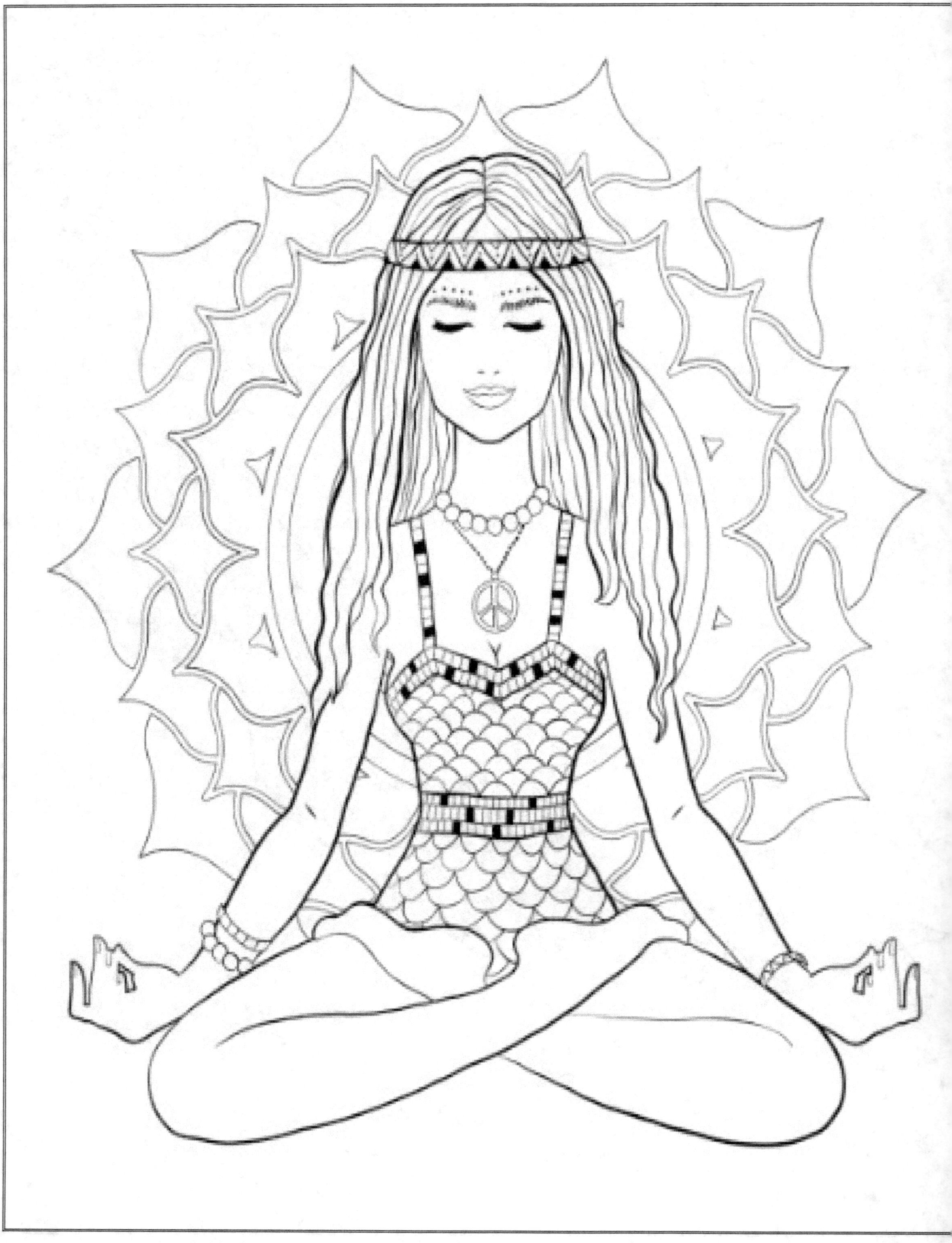

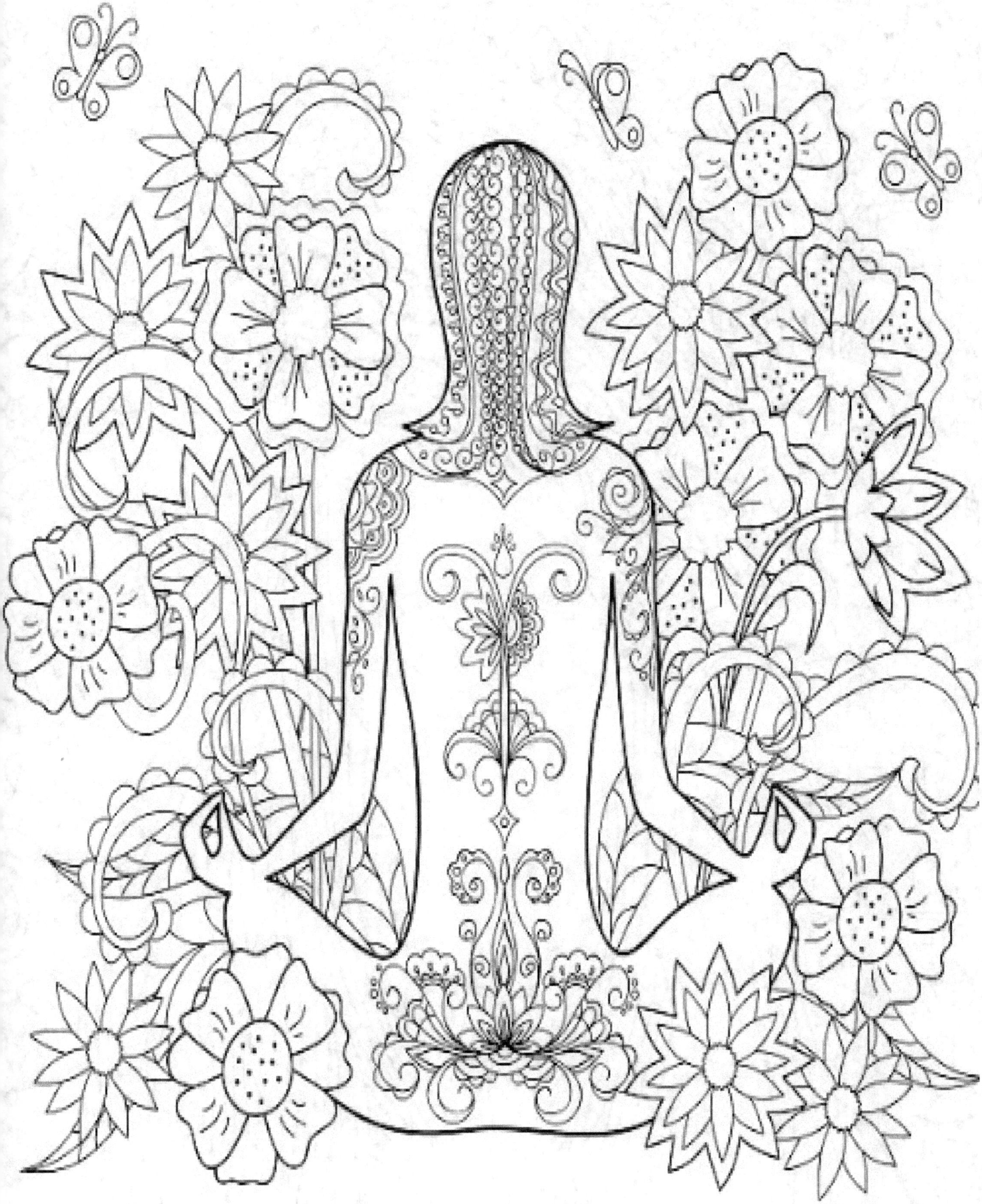

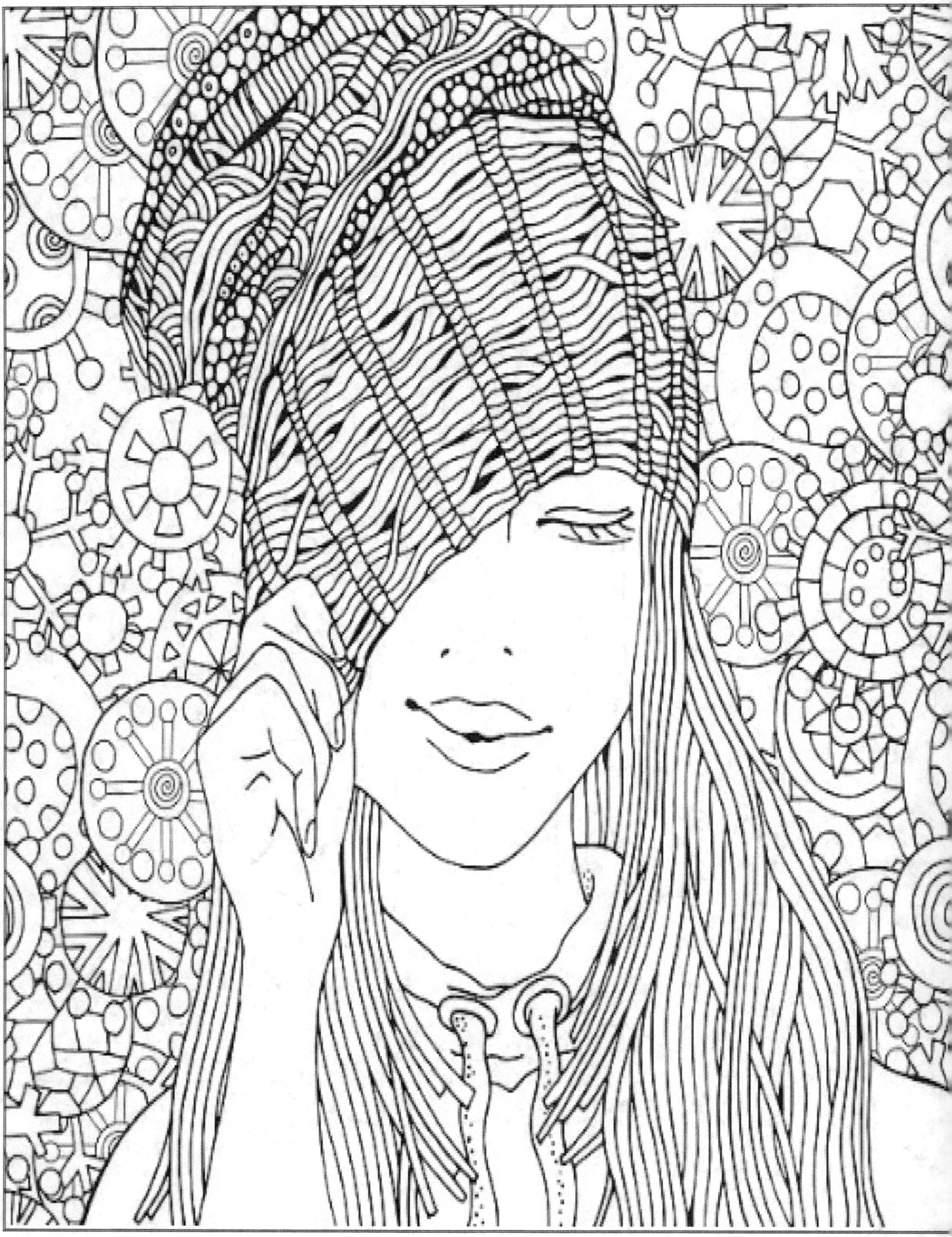

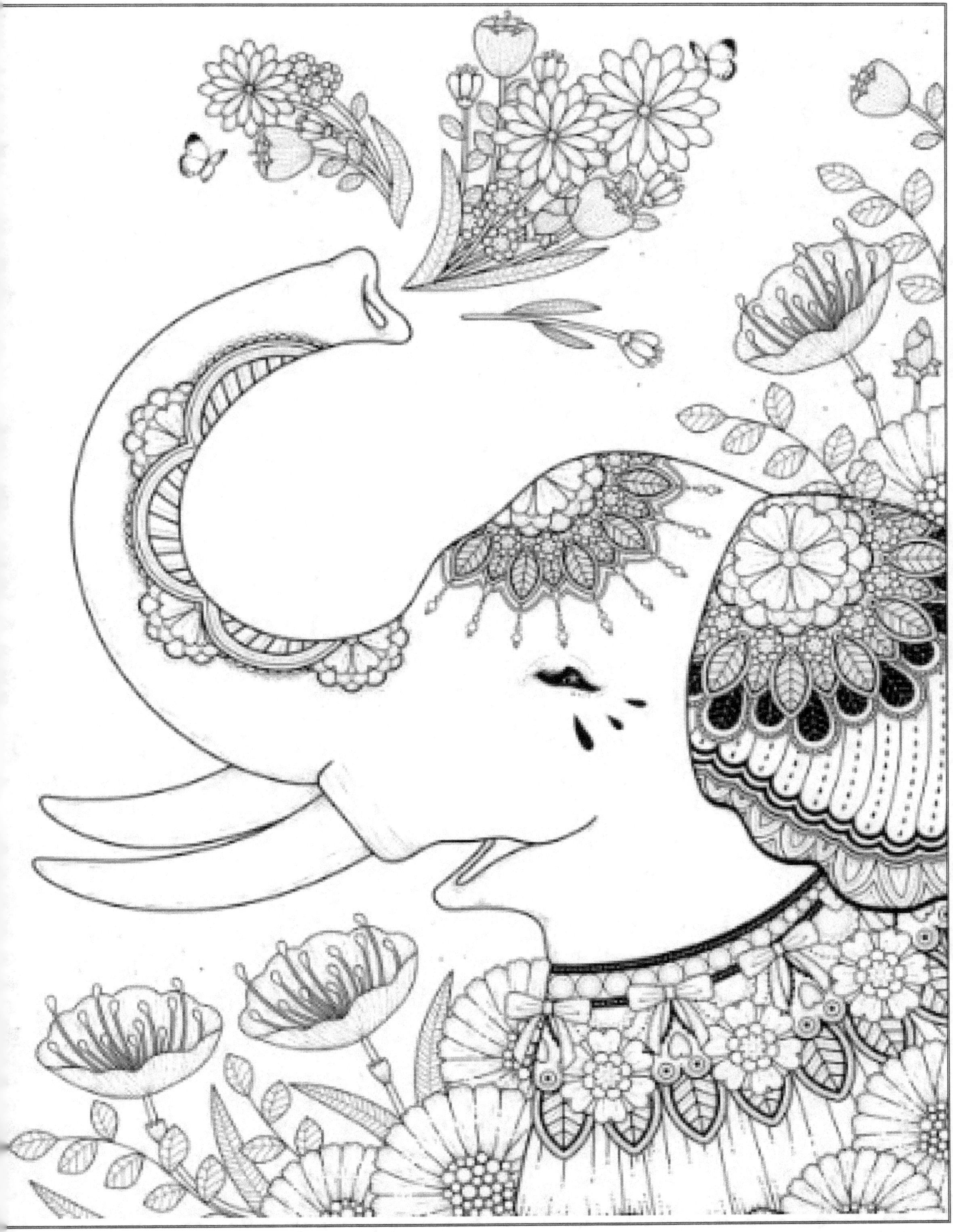

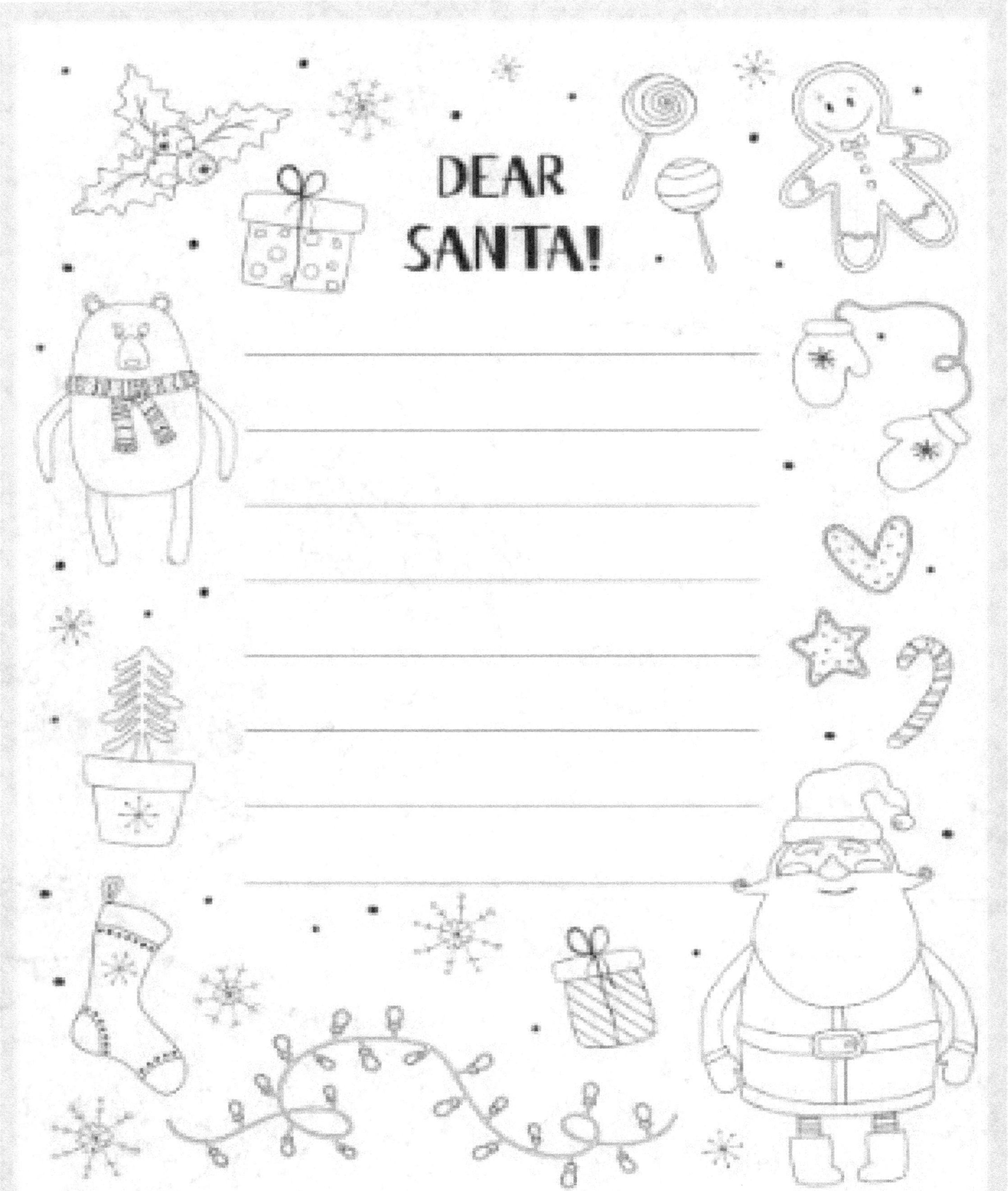
DEAR SANTA!

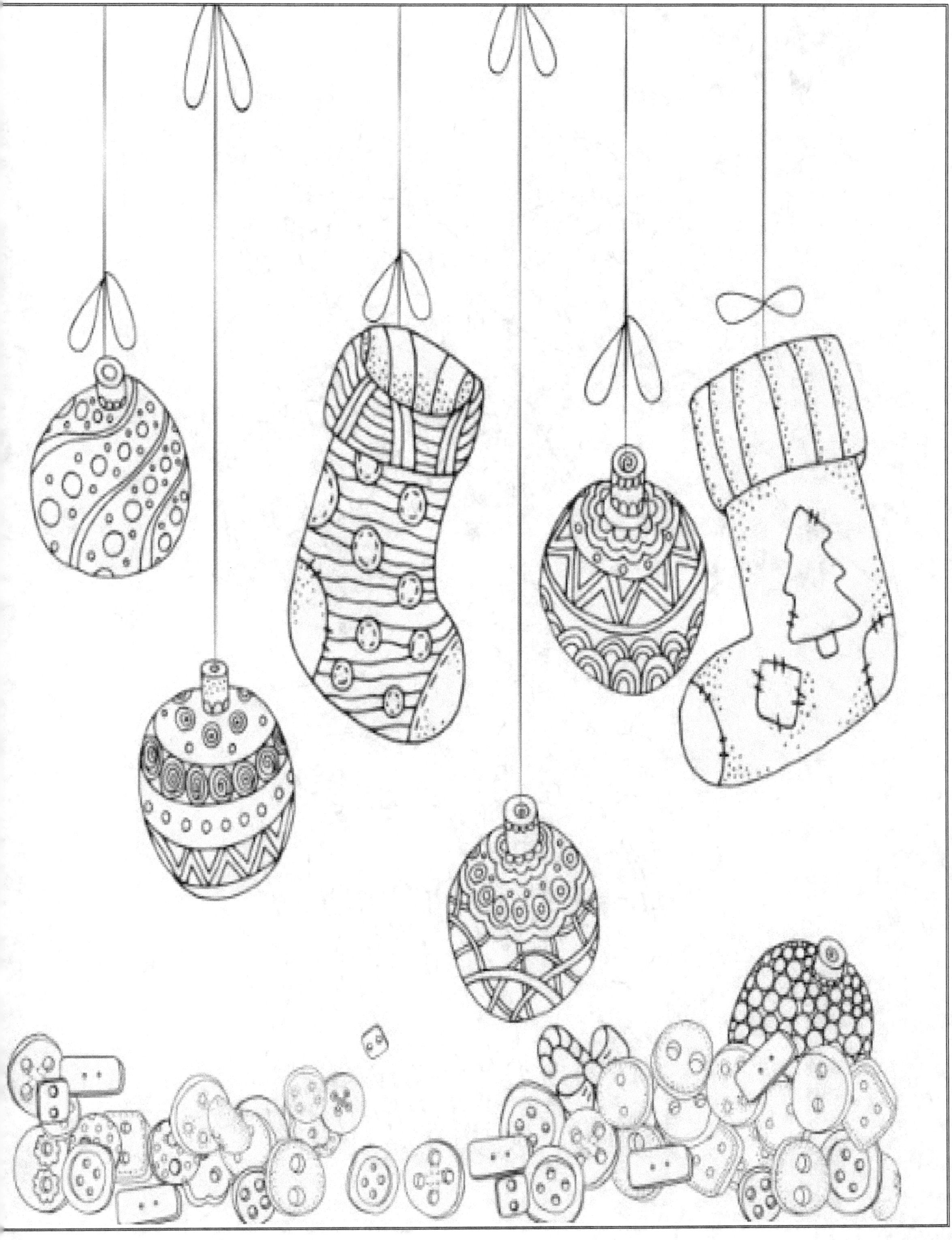

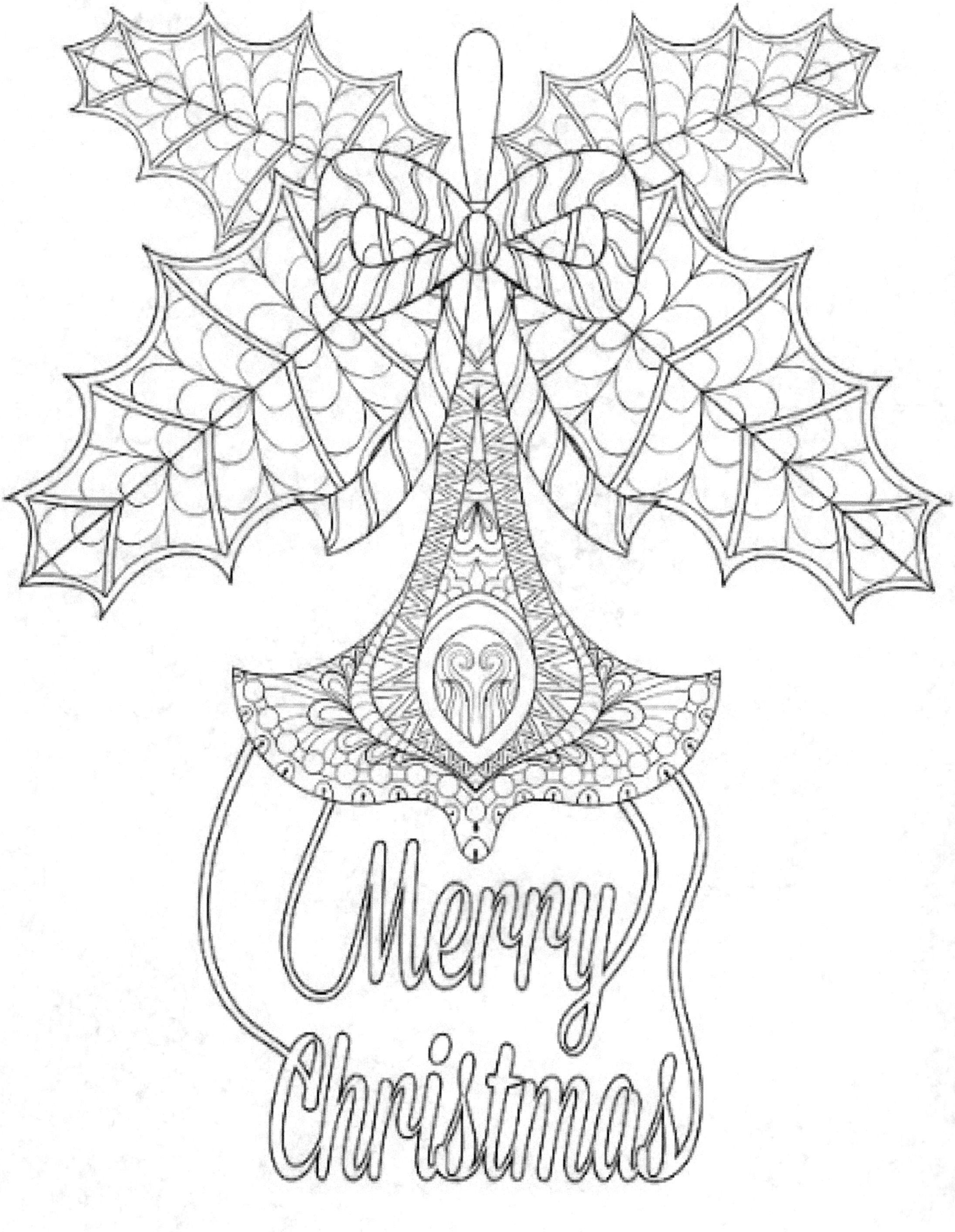
Merry
Christmas

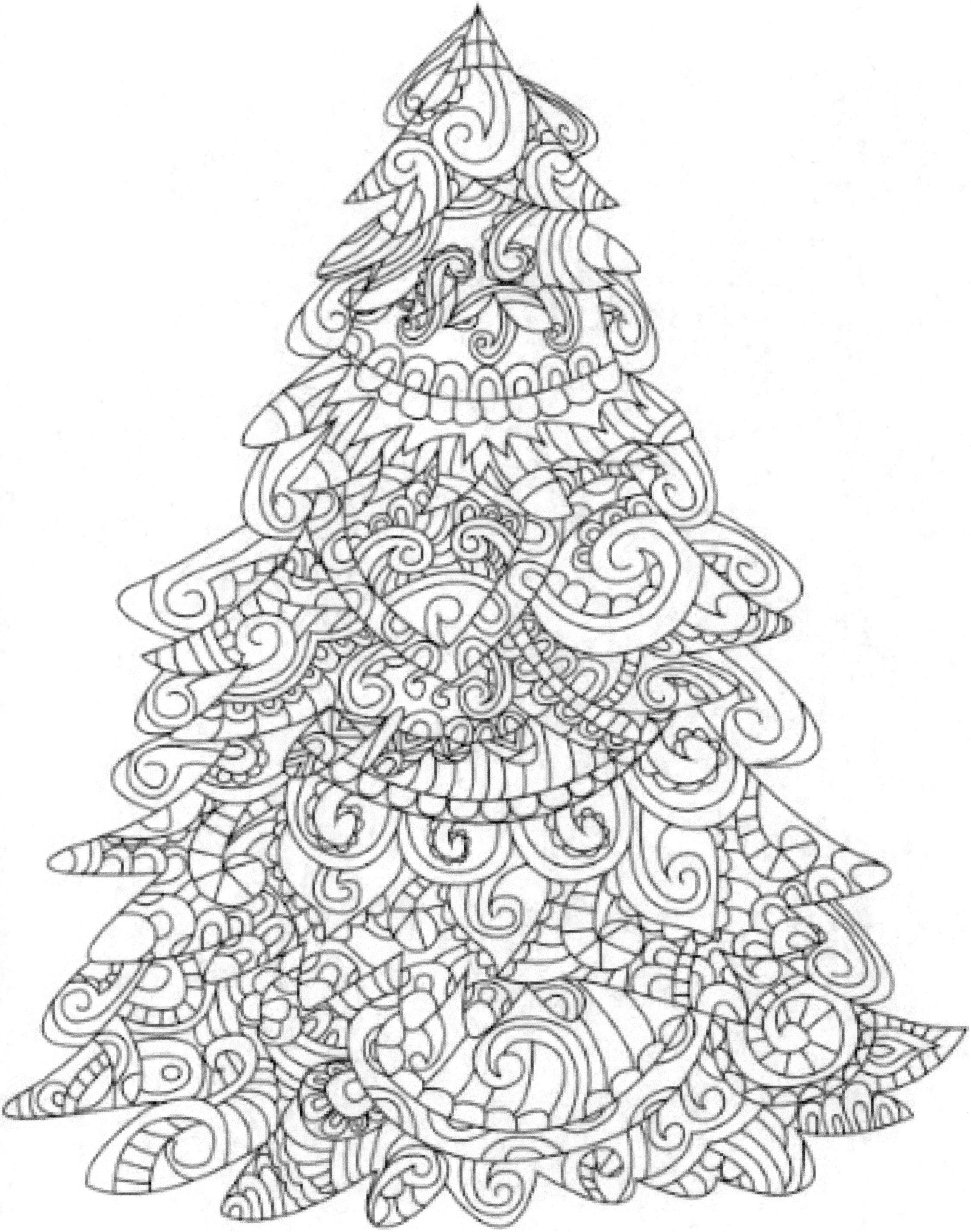

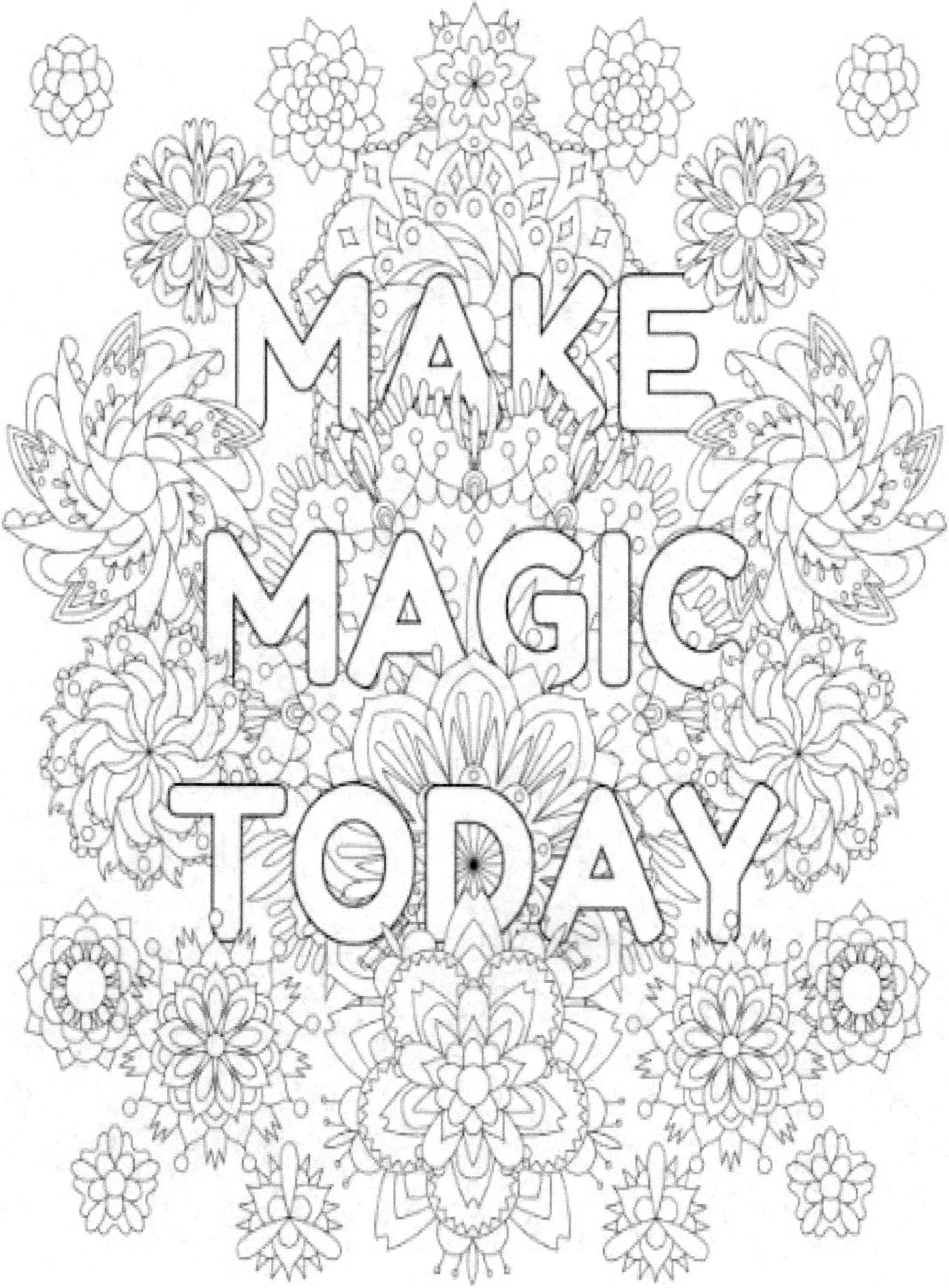
MAKE
MAGIC
TODAY

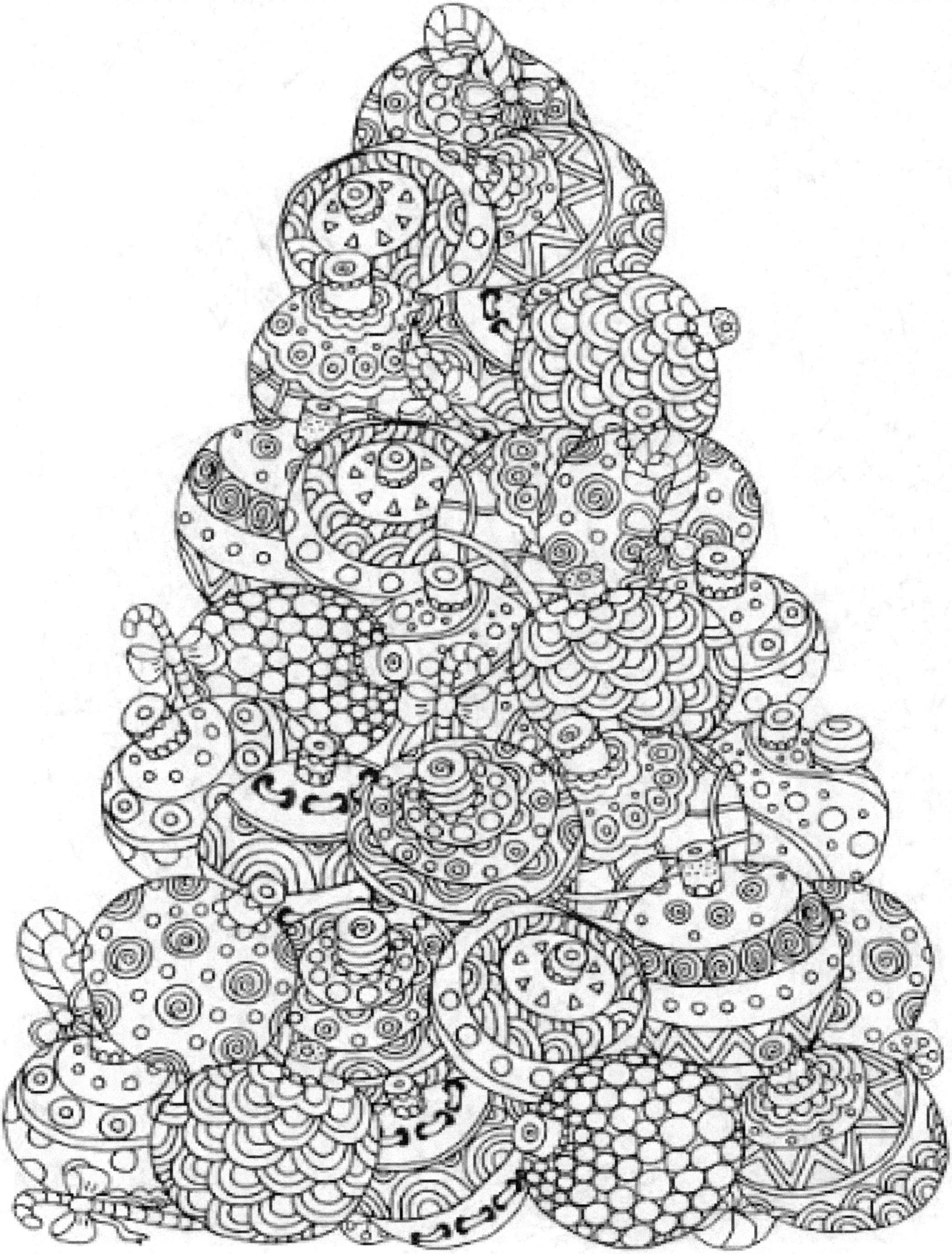

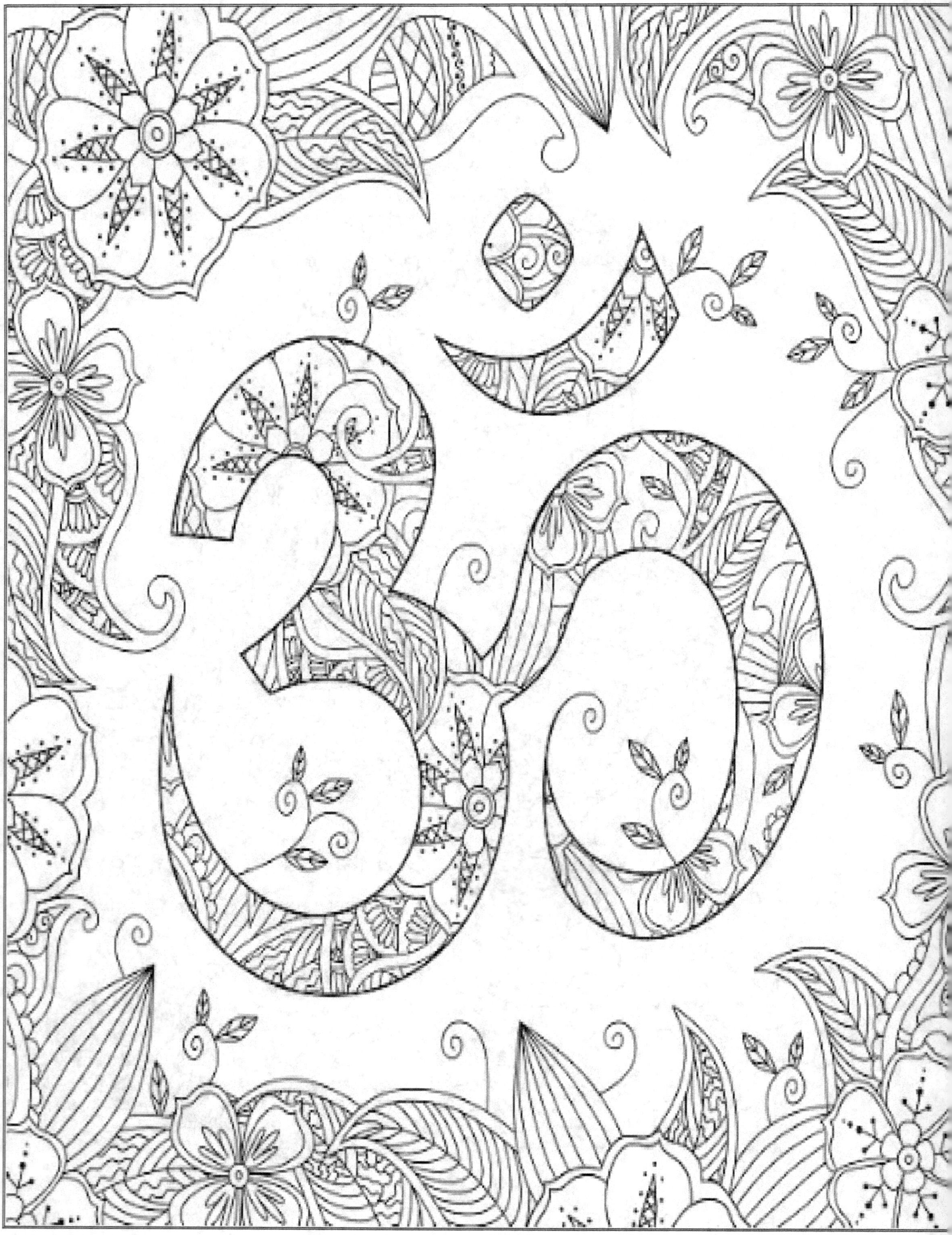

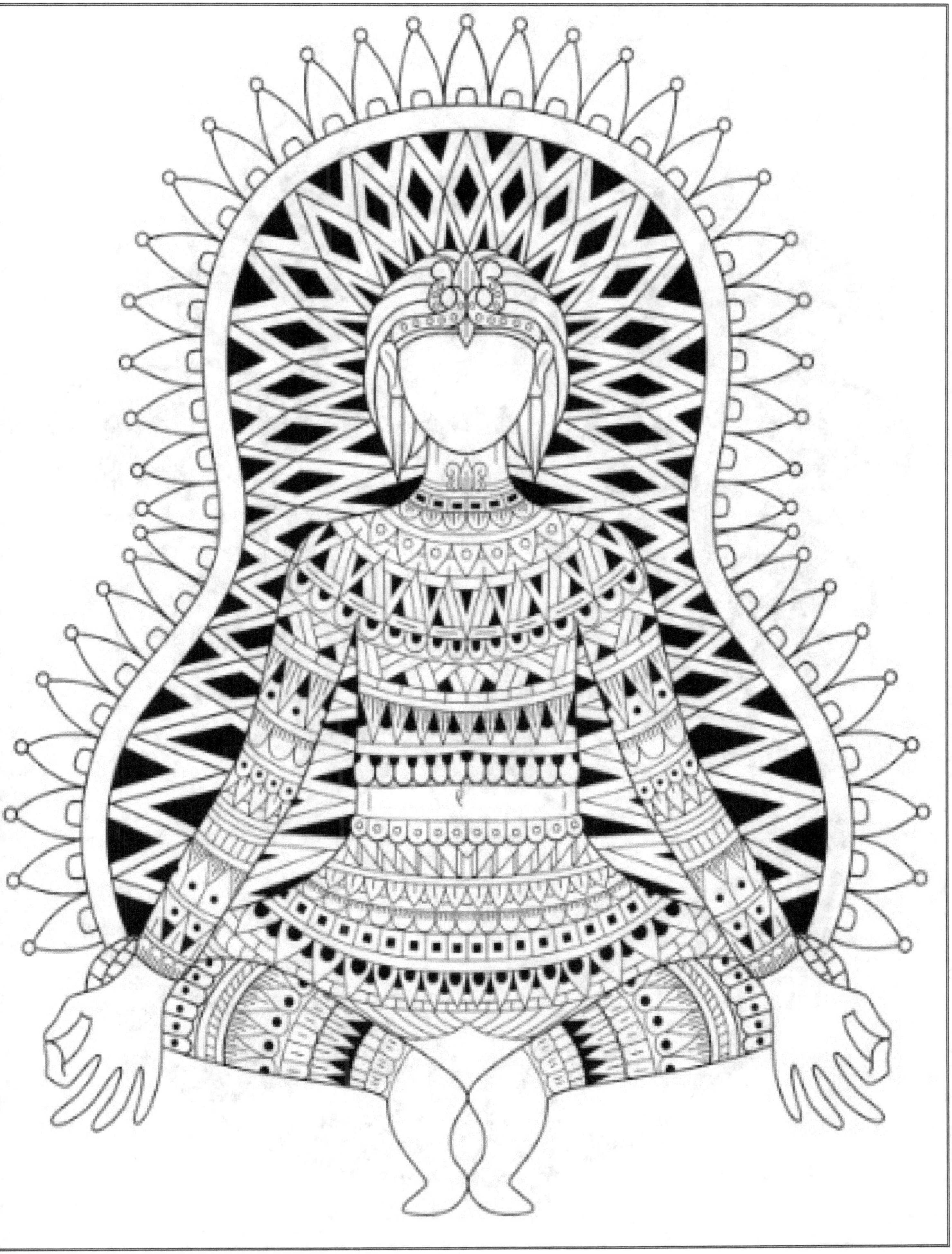

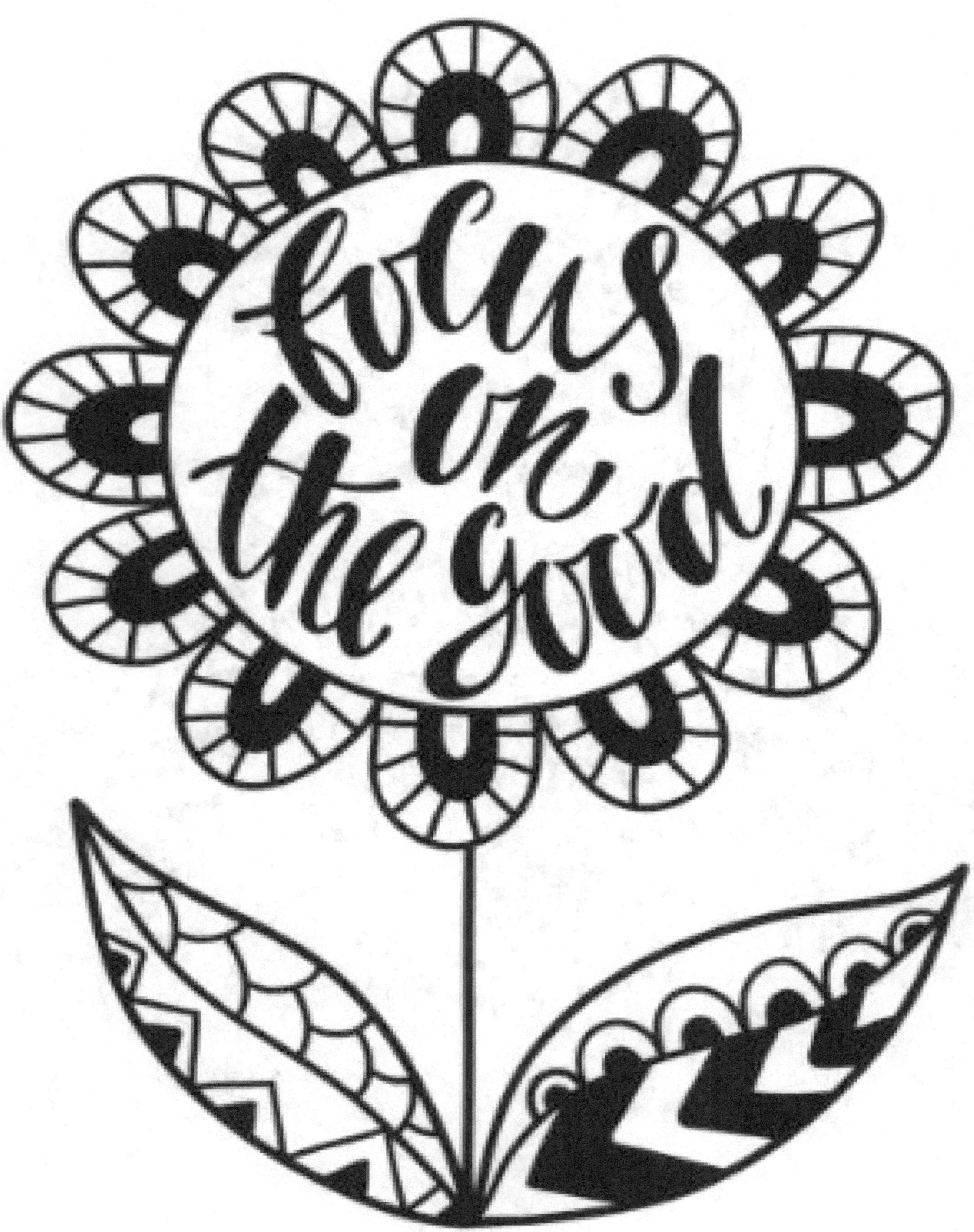
focus on the good

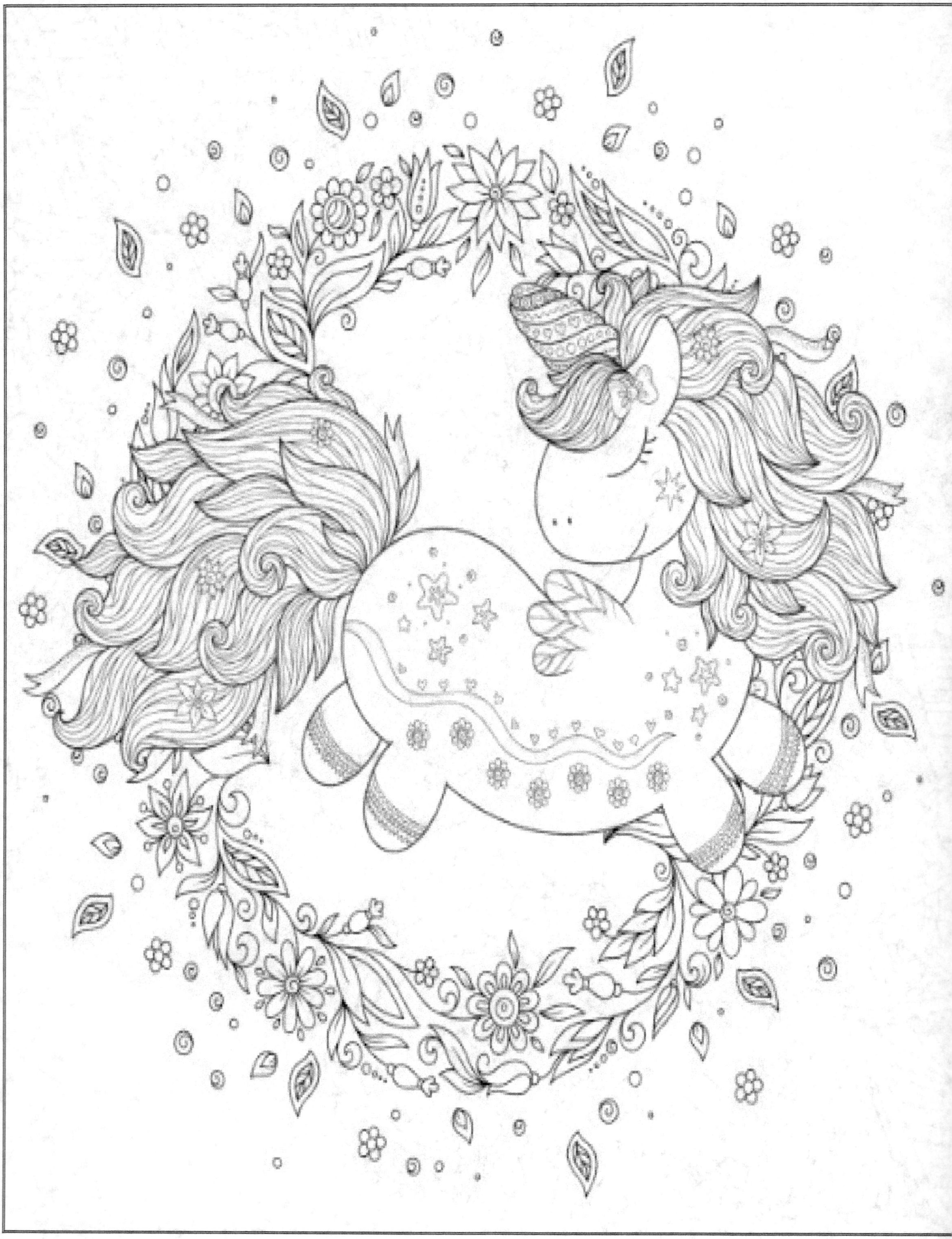

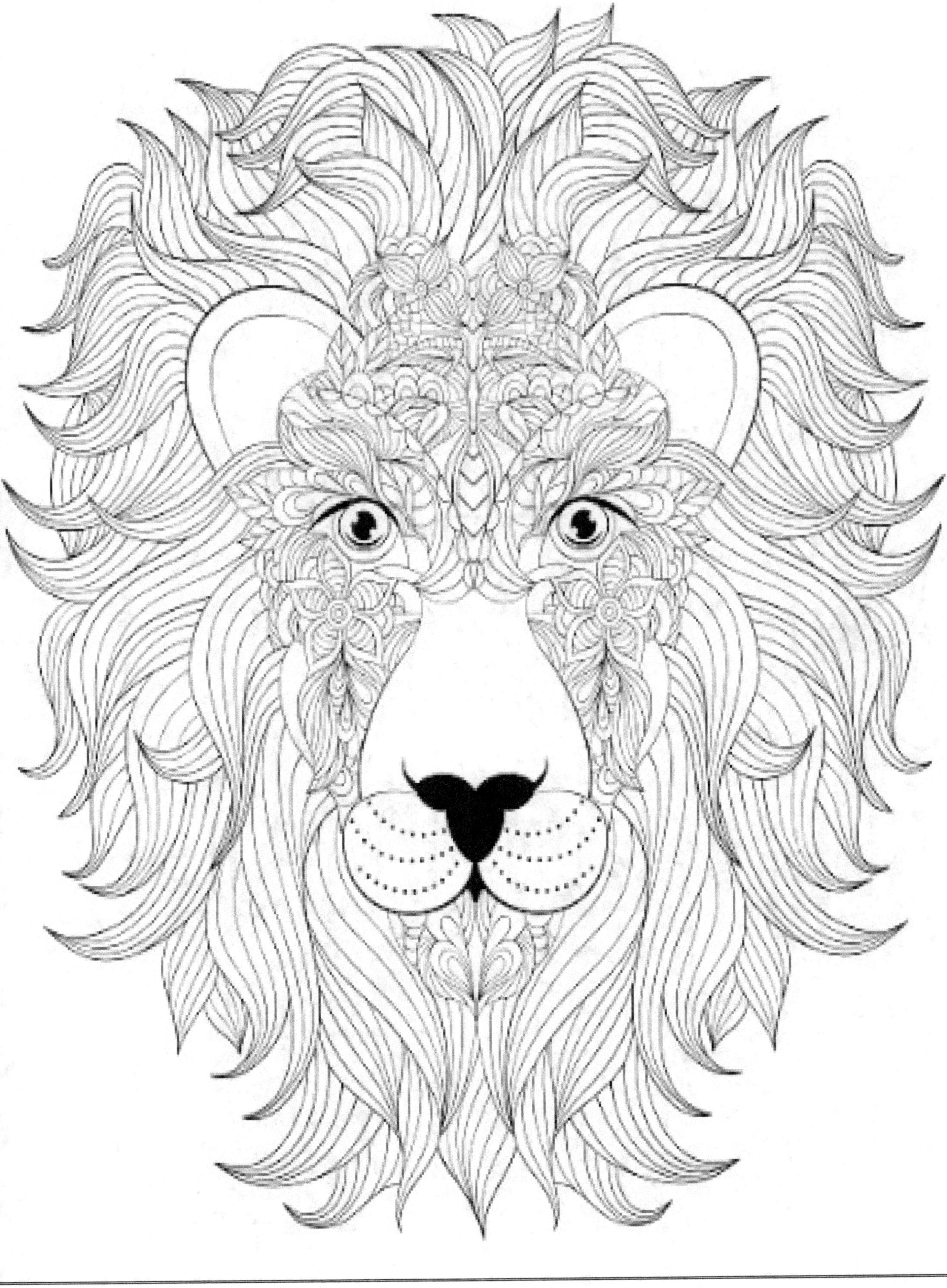

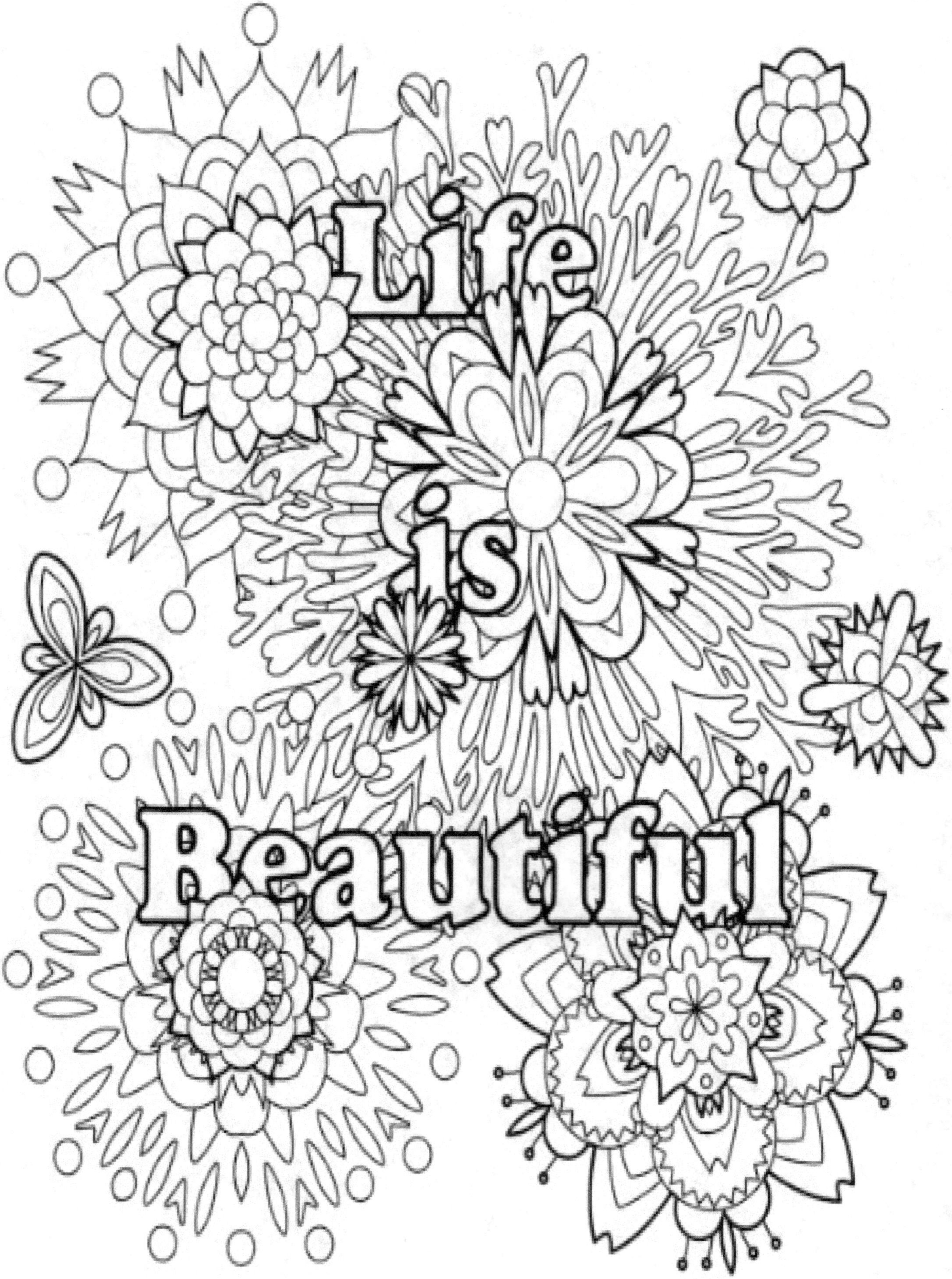
Life
is
Beautiful

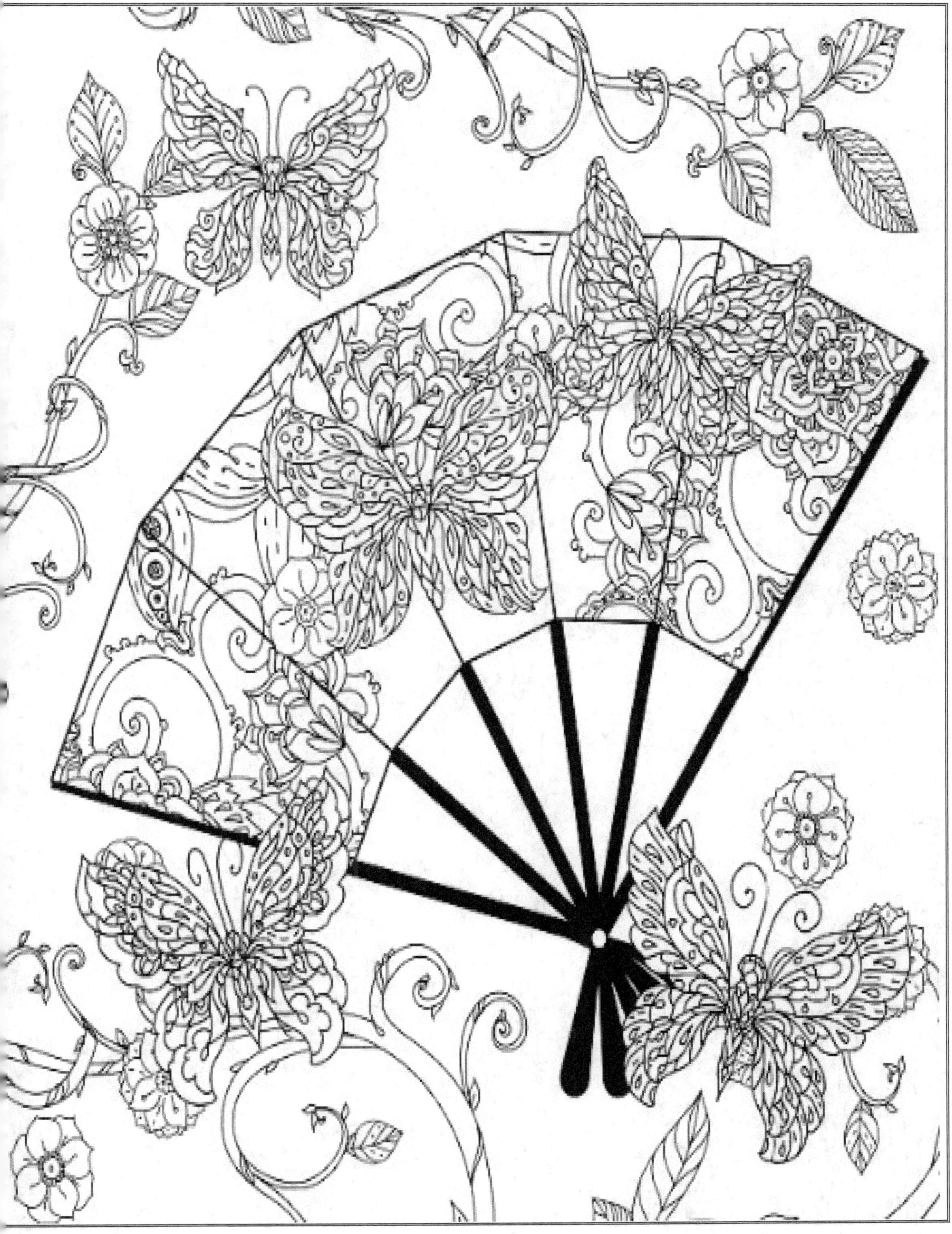

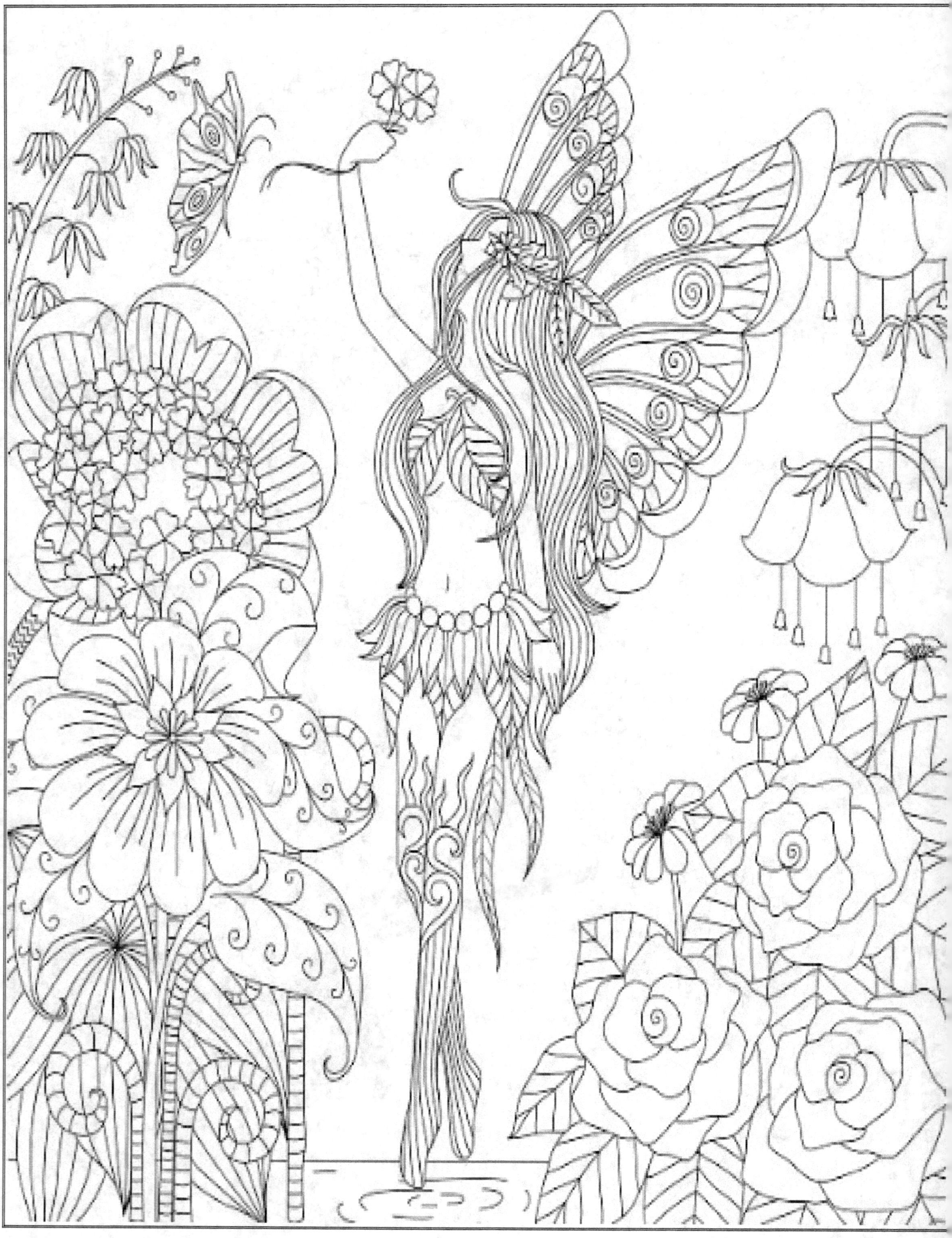

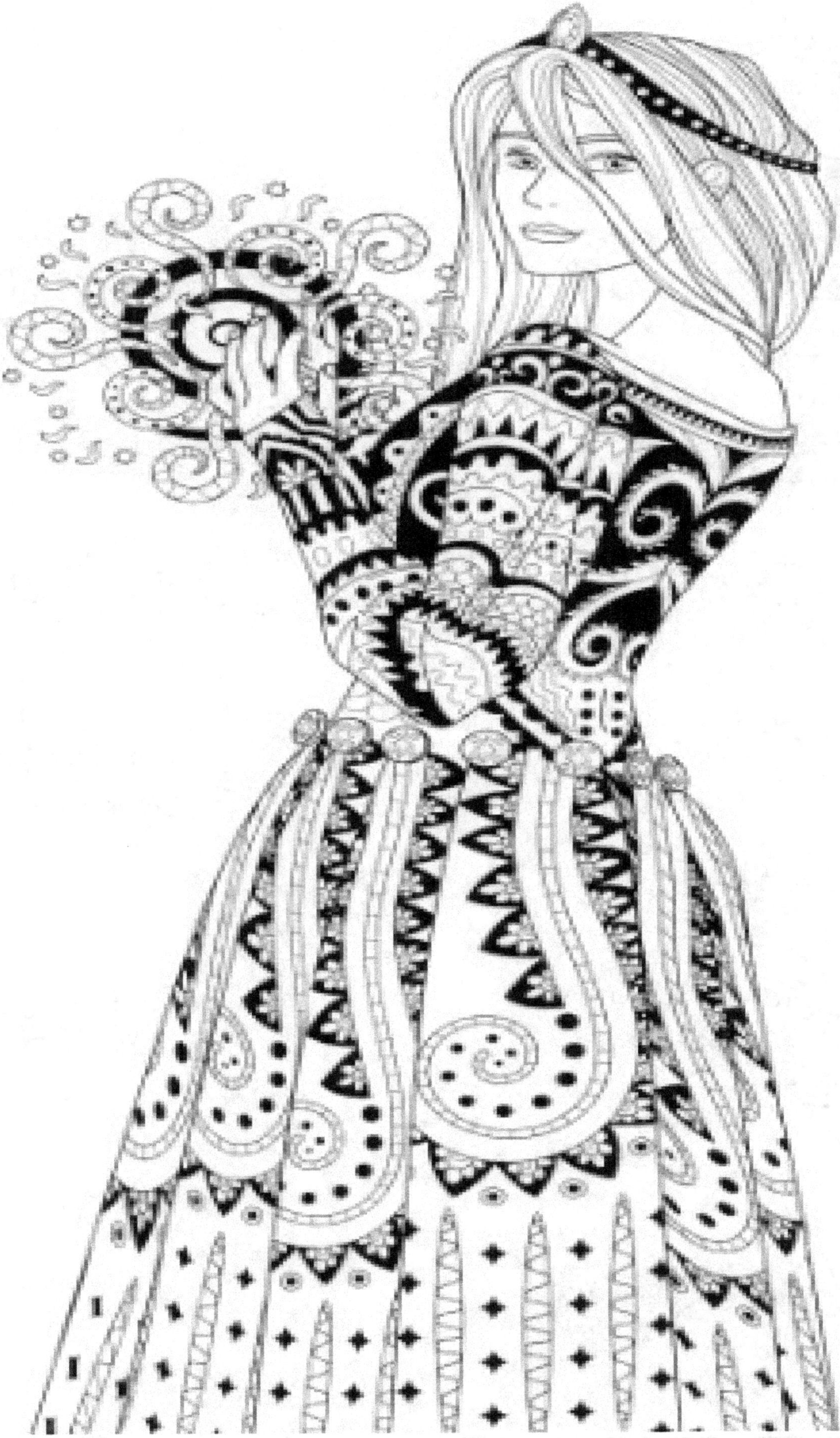

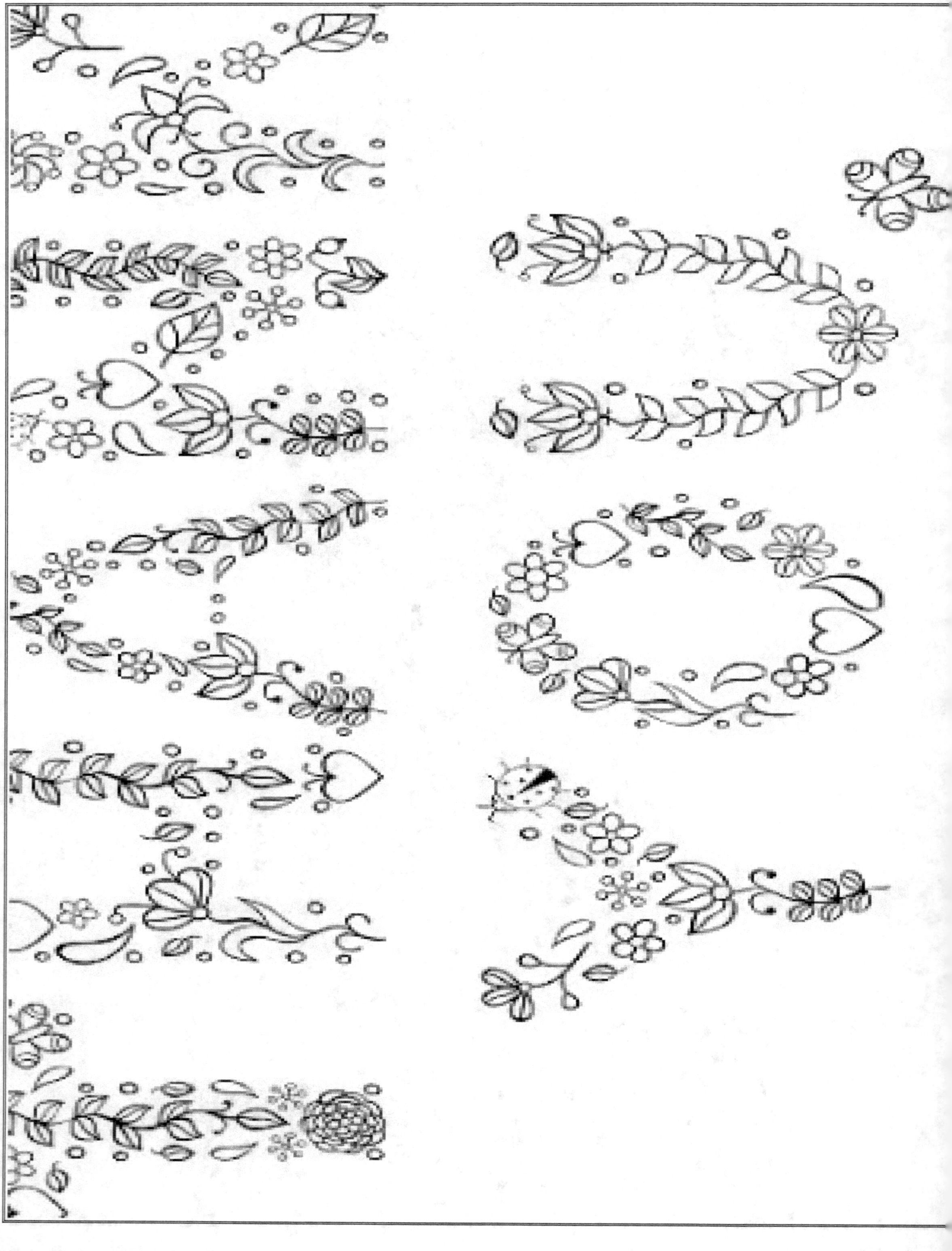

www.ingramcontent.com/pod-product-compliance
Lightning Source LLC
Chambersburg PA
CBHW080603220526
45466CB00010B/3233
* 9 7 9 8 5 3 0 7 5 6 9 6 2 *